DON'T LOOK AWAY

Embracing ANTI-BIAS Classrooms

Iheoma U. Iruka, PhD • Stephanie M. Curenton, PhD • Tonia R. Durden, PhD • Kerry-Ann Escayg, PhD

Gryphon House

LIBRARY OF CONGRESS
CATALOGING-IN-PUBLICATION DATA

Library of Congress Control Number:2019953929

BULK PURCHASE

Gryphon House books are available for special premiums and sales promotions as well as for fund-raising use. Special editions or book excerpts also can be created to specifications. For details, call 800.638.0928.

DISCLAIMER

Gryphon House, Inc., cannot be held responsible for damage, mishap, or injury incurred during the use of or because of activities in this book. Appropriate and reasonable caution and adult supervision of children involved in activities and corresponding to the age and capability of each child involved are recommended at all times. Do not leave children unattended at any time. Observe safety and caution at all times.

CONTENTS

ACKNOWLEDGMENTS

We stand on the shoulders of others who paved the way for us to be early childhood scholars, researchers, educators, and advocates for social justice. We thank our parents, spouses, and children, who continue to support our work, mission, and goal to ensure that our communities prosper and thrive while also dismantling racism, discrimination, and inequities. We thank all of the parents, families, children, communities and community leaders, colleagues, and organizations that have supported our research on supporting the well-being and achievement of Black children and other children of color.

INTRODUCTION

In this book, we seek to support program leaders, providers, teachers, and others who are interested in strengthening the early care and education sector to provide the best care and learning environment for all children. Most importantly, we seek to honor the history of early care and education, which started with President Lyndon Johnson's 1965 War on Poverty. That effort strived to ensure that poor children, the majority of whom were Black, were able to start school at the same level as their White peers. While early care and education has made great strides in creating supports for children's school and life success, there is still a long way to go when many children—especially Black children and other children of color—do not have the same access to high-quality early care and education programs as their White peers.

As you read, we will encourage you to think about your *unconscious biases* (those negative thoughts, feelings, and stereotypes we have that are outside our awareness) toward race, class, and gender identities. We all have them! In fact, left to their own devices, our brains will automatically create such biases, but it is our job to *actively control* our thinking by catching ourselves when our minds wander toward negative stereotypes. We must purposefully reteach our brains that those biases are not true. We will also encourage you to reflect on your past and present experiences, both inside and outside the classroom. We will encourage you to imagine what it would take to be an early childhood educator who strives to change the world by intentionally seeking to make the upcoming generations less biased and more inclusive toward marginalized and underrepresented populations due to race, ethnicity, language, sexual orientation, or gender identity. We challenge you to take action by speaking up and advocating for the rights of children and aiming to influence those policies and practices that have children's well-being in mind.

Early childhood educators have a pivotal role in changing the future, because the early years of life, birth to age eight, are the most critical time period in our human development. These early years are a sensitive period for the growth of children's language, self-regulation, cognition, physical development, moral development, and self-identity. When children experience trauma caused by toxic stress and negative life events, including stress caused by bias and racism, the consequences can continue into later life. Even though children are resilient in the face of many adversities, early childhood professionals can make the road a little smoother, especially for those children who face a lot of bumps, bruises, and hardships due to their race, ethnicity, culture, language, or religion. Research has taught us about the lifelong benefit of early childhood education, but we are also learning about the lifelong impact of trauma, especially when it is experienced during this sensitive period of development.

One such trauma experienced by young children, especially children of color, is exclusion. Often, this takes the form of suspension and expulsion. Two hundred and fifty children are suspended from school every day, and many of them are children of color. When we consider the achievement gap and third-grade reading scores, we realize that these are the children who need education and support the most. Children of color are not experiencing high-quality early learning the same way or at the same rate as White children. (We will discuss this further in chapter 2.)

It is urgent that we deliver on the promise of equal education by providing equitable early care and education. To do this, we must address bias, racism, segregation, low expectations, and trauma, and ensure that early care and education programs and educators are engaging in culturally responsive anti-bias education with children, especially Black children and other children of color.

HOW TO USE THIS BOOK

The authors aim to provide a resource to help those working with or on behalf of children. We seek to unpack and address the implicit biases (also known as unconscious biases) that paint how we treat and see each other and the biases that harm children, whether intentionally or unintentionally. For example, how do you perceive a mother who is always ten minutes late in dropping off or picking up her child? How does this behavior influence how you see this child? Does your perception change if this mother has similar attributes to you or your mother? What if you know the lateness in the morning is due to the father who wants to spend a few minutes with his son because he works the graveyard shift (10 p.m.–8 a.m.) every day? What is the emotional harm done to a Black child when he is often getting the message that he is scary and no one wants him around? What is the emotional harm done to young girls who are told they are too loud and have too much attitude? Are we laying a foundation that ensures they will be successful or one that says there is something wrong with them?

This book seeks to support early educators in recognizing, addressing, and eliminating bias and in practicing culturally responsive, anti-bias pedagogies to ensure that trauma is not being revisited upon the children we are expected to protect, nurture, and educate. In each chapter, the author of that chapter offers information and research to help you understand and recognize bias. We discuss anti-bias education and culturally responsive pedagogy to give you the tools to teach children equitably. And, we offer questions for reflection, to help you think critically about bias and ways to implement culturally responsive practices and anti-bias pedagogy.

You can use this book as a personal exercise to develop your own understanding, or in a community of practice, or as professional development with staff. We hope the information we provide will help you see the children in your care with new eyes as you do the very important work of nurturing and encouraging them and preparing them for success in the future.

DON'T LOOK AWAY: EMBRACING ANTI-BIAS CLASSROOMS

CHAPTER 1

EARLY CHILDHOOD EDUCATION'S ROOTS IN SOCIAL JUSTICE

This chapter examines how early childhood became part of the national discourse on social justice through its establishment during the War on Poverty and how this lens of socioeconomic and social justice continues to be woven through early education.

THE REALITY OF IMPLICIT BIAS

"What could it be this time?" Dr. Regina Williamson sighs and puts her palm on her forehead as she looks at the number on her cellphone. Her son Reginald's child-care program, Promise Academy Child Development Center, is calling. She wonders what they could be calling her about in the less than 30 minutes since she dropped off her two sons. This is the third call in three weeks! The other two calls had forced her to cancel her office hours with students to rush to pick up one of the boys because the school indicated he was being aggressive with other children. She quickly looks at her calendar to see what appointments she would need to cancel.

Regina breathes a long, overwhelmed sigh. She and her husband have worked hard to provide their boys with the best education possible. They want their sons to be understood and well-liked by the teachers and students; this isn't always easy, given that the boys are typically the only African American children in predominantly White preschools. She knows it can't just be her boys, because she has heard other moms in the school talking about how their own children behave. They behave even worse than Reginald and Dawaan, yet they don't get suspended. What is it about her boys? It just seems as though the teachers are too hard on them.

She slowly answers her cellphone. "Hello, Ms. Shaunda."

These are questions that often ring in the minds of many Black parents. What could and should they be doing to make sure their children, especially boys, are not being suspended? Should they put them on medication to control their behavior? Should they just find relative care or homeschool their children? The truth is that even if Black parents medicate their children or pay for a behavioral specialist, there is still a high likelihood that their children will be suspended or excluded from learning for the same behaviors that barely register when White boys do it. Why is this the case? Both research and the lived experiences of Black families and other families of color indicate that Reginald and Dawaan receive inequitable experiences because they are Black and because their behaviors are seen as more threatening and uncontrollable compared to White boys.

A seminal study conducted by Yale researcher Walter Gilliam asked early education teachers to watch a video in which a Black boy, a Black girl, a White boy, and a White girl were seated at a table (Gilliam et al., 2016). The teachers were told that they would see children misbehaving and were asked to press a button when they saw a misbehavior. (Unbeknownst to the teachers, there were no misbehaviors from any of the children.) Teachers of all races pressed the button the most for Black children, indicating that the children were misbehaving. As part of the study, the teachers wore eye trackers so the researchers could collect data on where the teachers were looking. The data indicated that teachers were more likely to watch the Black children, especially the Black boy. This shows that the teachers were thinking that the Black boy was most likely to misbehave.

After participating in the study, the teachers were informed that the children actually were actors and that they were not misbehaving at all. When the teachers were asked why they thought the Black children misbehaved the most, they indicated they pressed the button because they thought they saw misbehavior or they anticipated a particular problem. For example, when the Black boy asked to share a toy, the teachers anticipated that he would become mad and aggressive in the near future. This video provides some level of confirmation for US Department of Education data that show Black public-preschool children are 3.6 times more likely than their White counterparts to receive one or more out-of-school suspensions (US Department of Education, Office for Civil Rights, 2014). Black children represent only 18 percent of preschool enrollment but represent 48 percent of preschool children who receive one or more out-of-school

Implicit bias: a set of automatic and uncontrolled cognitive processes that affect our attitudes toward others. These biases are thought to be involuntary and not under the conscious control of the individual and can lead to either favorable or unfavorable characterizations of others.

suspensions. In comparison, White children represent 41 percent of preschool enrollment but only 28 percent of such children receiving one or more out-of-school suspensions. This disparity makes it clear that Black children are overrepresented in expulsion and suspension. The data have led researchers and many others to conclude that the reason for this is implicit, or unconscious, bias.

Perceptions of People of Color

For centuries, Black and other non-White peoples, including indigenous populations, have been viewed as less than human and even animal-like in some instances, incapable of emotions, intelligence, and social skills. This perception has been the rationale for enslavement, internment camps, and genocide. The legacy of viewing people of color as threatening continues today in representations of these groups as criminal, dangerous, lazy, and unintelligent. Therefore, early childhood educators who see young Black boys as threatening, dangerous, and incapable of learning can view suspension and expulsion as reasonable courses of action.

Implicit bias is a set of automatic and uncontrolled cognitive processes that affect our attitudes toward others. These biases are thought to be involuntary and not under the conscious control of the individual and can lead to either favorable or unfavorable characterizations of others. Implicit biases can result in stereotyping along dimensions such as class, race, ethnicity, appearance, age, sexuality, religion, or disability. Implicit bias can be seen, for example, when we spend time talking to people who are similar to us and avoid those who don't seem like us. It can be seen when teachers allow White children the independence to choose their work but don't provide those choices for Black children because they worry that Black children may become uncontrollable. It is very important to stress that implicit bias is unconscious to the offender but is often obvious to the victim and may have deep and lasting effects. These biases and lack of learning opportunities for Black children are not what early program designers and administrators were thinking or worried about when they designed early childhood programs such as Head Start. While we all engage in biased behaviors, and many people face different experiences of bias, in this book we are particularly focused on and sensitive to the bias, racism, discrimination, and exclusionary practices against children, families, and communities of color, especially those of Black children. Bias against Black people is particularly salient and pervasive.

HEAD START'S ROLE IN EQUITABLE LEARNING OPPORTUNITIES

In his first State of the Union address in 1964, President Lyndon Johnson proposed the Economic Opportunity Act (EOA), which we now refer to as the War on Poverty (Zigler and Valentine, 1979). At the time of this proposal, there was a 19 percent poverty rate among families in the United States. The legislation established the Office of Economic Opportunity, which housed numerous programs designed to alleviate poverty, such as VISTA (now known as AmeriCorps VISTA), Job Corps (offering free education and vocational training to people sixteen to twenty-four years of age), and Head Start. Head Start was conceived as a community-based early childhood program intended to provide comprehensive services—cognitive, emotional, social, health, and nutrition—to preschool-age children from low-income households. As a former teacher in a one-room schoolhouse in Texas, President Johnson believed in the power of education to eradicate poverty.

At its inception in 1965, Head Start was an eight-week summer program located in community child-development centers throughout the country and serving more than 560,000 children (Administration for Children and Families, n.d.). Today, Head Start is a full-day, full-year program and serves infants and toddlers (in Early Head Start) as well as preschoolers (Bosland et al., 2011; Zigler, Gilliam, and Barnett, 2011). The War on Poverty legislation reminds us that, to truly support children, we must support their families as comprehensively as possible and not focus on just the child or the parent.

> *As Regina drives to her sons' child-care program, she continues to think through the conversation she just had with Ms. Shaunda. The words keep ringing in her head: "Reginald is a big, hulking, five-year-old kid" (even though Reginald is three years old). Ms. Shaunda went on to explain that he may need to be in a different school that "fits his needs."*

She wonders what she and her husband can do to stop their sons' aggressive behavior in school. The boys are never aggressive at home. She starts thinking about who among her friends she could call on to help her find a therapist. She thinks about all the child-care programs her sons have gone to, from ones housed on the university campus where she works to others that were close to her family's home. She knows her boys can be boisterous, but she has never thought they were aggressive children.

As Regina continues her drive to her sons' child-care program, she also thinks about how finding new care is going to impact her family and her job. She worries about how Reginald will feel about having to change schools again and the stress he would feel with no longer seeing his friends and teachers. Mothers are supposed to protect their children and keep them safe, but Regina wonders how she can protect them in a world that sees them as angry, older, and Black.

Reflection Questions

> What is the responsibility of the teacher and the school in creating responsive environments for all their students?

> Think about Ms. Shaunda's perception of Black boys. What are the historical roots of such representations? How do those perceptions play out in contemporary life? Studies have noted that many teachers view Black boys as more threatening and older than they actually are, and often anticipate that they will become aggressive and angry, even if that is not the case.

> What are the mechanisms that allowed for such representations to be so pervasive in American society? Also consider, for what purpose did they develop?

> Consider your calls or texts with parents. Do you typically contact parents to share good news or bad news about their child?

> Which families do you often call or text with bad news? Are they families of color or those with boys?

> Are there one or two children you often have problems with? Who are they, and why do you think you have a problem with them?

WAR ON POVERTY AS AN ACT OF SOCIAL JUSTICE

The intention of Johnson's War on Poverty was to ensure that poor and racially minoritized children were protected from the negative effects of poverty and were set on a pathway that ensured they were academically successful and would become productive citizens. Also part of Johnson's plan, the Elementary and Secondary Education Act (ESEA) was enacted in 1965 to provide funding, training, and other supports to schools serving children from low-income families. The goal of both Head Start and ESEA, and now of most early education programs, is to reduce achievement gaps between poor and non-poor children and to provide all students with high-quality, equitable education. Part of reducing the achievement gap was to address the needs of children prior to entering kindergarten, especially for children from poor households. More than fifty years ago, people recognized the need for proactive actions to eliminate poverty by providing educational opportunities, especially for children from disadvantaged families, and for preschool programs and services to ensure that children enter kindergarten prepared to learn and benefit from school. Current research suggests that children from low-income families benefit from having access to high-quality health and dental care, supplemental food assistance, and behavioral health services. With these supports, the potential for success and long-term positive outcomes for children and families are maximized (Bosland, et al., 2011; Zigler, Gilliam, and Barnett, 2011).

Minority: a group of people who make up less than half of the total number of people

Minoritized: a group of people having little power or representation relative to other groups within a society

Johnson's War on Poverty was an act of social justice. *Social justice* can be defined as "the active promotion of a just society by challenging systemic and institutional racism, inequality, and oppression." In the 1960s, many families of color were living in poverty and were not provided with equal opportunities to be successful. Initiatives like

Social justice: the active promotion of a just society by challenging systemic and institutional racism, inequality, and oppression

the War on Poverty were attempts to fix the injustices of slavery, Jim Crow, redlining, and many other institutionalized laws and policies that oppressed and discriminated against minority people, especially Black people. While many historical policies, such as housing and employment discrimination, are being corrected, the legacy of how Black people (and other people of color) are often seen and treated in society has not been effectively acknowledged and addressed (Castle et al., 2019). We see this in Dr. Williamson's case where her sons are often seen as threatening and older, which has an impact on the children and the family.

Redlining: systematic denial of services, such as banking, health care, and insurance, to residents of specific, often racially associated, neighborhoods or communities, either directly or through selectively raising prices

Head Start seeks to support children's school readiness and to sustain their development and learning into kindergarten and beyond by supporting families. Head Start's Parent, Family, Community Engagement Framework (US Department of Health and Human Services, 2011) focuses on ways to achieve these goals through measures such as:

> - Family well-being
> - Parent-child relationships
> - Families as lifelong educators
> - Families as learners
> - Family engagement in transitions
> - Family connections to peers and community
> - Families as advocates and leaders

Thus, Head Start has a three-pronged focus: providing high-quality educational experiences for children, equipping families to support their children's learning, and supporting families in becoming more economically secure. When these goals are achieved, families thrive.

In the vein of social justice, many Head Start programs are mandated to engage with their local communities to link families with resources and to increase programs' capacity to serve the needs of families and children. Arguably, some early childhood programs not affiliated with Head Start are also equitable, offer high-quality education, and meet the holistic needs of the children in their care. These programs also have a mission to create both comprehensive services and educational experiences for children. Therefore, as we begin these discussions focused on social justice in early childhood, think about how your program and services reflect (or do not reflect) these core values and impacts on young children and families.

Reflection Questions

> How do your program and services reflect (or not reflect) core values of equitable, high-quality education, equipping families to support their children's learning, and supporting families in becoming more economically secure?

> How can we ensure that families like the Williamsons are able to receive the promise of what high-quality early care and education can provide?

As a federal program, Head Start, along with the rigorously designed early intervention programs such as the HighScope Perry Preschool and Carolina Abecedarian programs, created the early learning foundation, research evidence, and policy push to provide safe, healthy, and cognitively stimulating early care and education programs, especially for children from low-income families or families facing adverse circumstances. The common threads among effective early education programs are leadership; low child-to-staff ratios; small group size; educated, trained, and well-paid teachers and personnel; developmentally appropriate curricula and learning standards; family engagement; and use of data to inform teacher practices and program implementation (Minervino, 2014). In sum, the best programs are those that treat every child as special and see the potential inherent in each of them. Furthermore, there is a need to recognize that the Perry Preschool and Abecedarian studies, as well as Head Start, started primarily with Black children and families. This is not an indication that there is something inherently wrong with Black children and families; however, it should highlight the racism that continues to perpetuate keeping Black families and other families of color in generational poverty.

making sure a child is cared for no matter the circumstances

HighScope Perry Preschool Program

The HighScope Perry Preschool Program (PPP) started in 1962 in Ypsilanti, Michigan, with a focus on serving three- and four-year-olds in a center-based program with a home-visiting component. The program primarily served Black children and their families. It focused on promoting children's social, language, and cognitive skills through hands-on play with a specially trained teacher. Children were in the program for one to two years. An experimental study showed that, compared with children not enrolled in the program, those who had been enrolled had higher academic grades and earnings, higher rates of high school graduation, fewer out-of-wedlock births, and lower levels of welfare receipt (Schweinhart et al., 2005). As adults, children in the PPP had fewer health problems compared to children who were not in the program (Heckman and Karapakula, 2019).

By Participating in these Programs these children and family had better health & life outcomes

Carolina Abecedarian Project

The Abecedarian Project (ABC) was a center-based intervention conducted with infants and preschool-age children through the Frank Porter Graham Child Development Institute in Chapel Hill, North Carolina. The families in the study were low income and headed by mostly single Black mothers with less than a high school education. ABC was a full-day, year-round program with a comprehensive curriculum focused on educational games supporting children's cognition, language, and behavior. ABC also focused on health and family support to meet the individualized needs of children and their families. In addition to performing better on academic measures, children who participated in the ABC study were more likely to complete college and be employed and were less likely to use public assistance and be young parents (Campbell et al., 2012). As adults, these children had fewer health problems than those who had not participated in the ABC program (Ramey, 2018).

Dr. Regina Williamson is a full-time professor, and her husband works full-time as a food inspector for a state agency. While they have some flexibility in their schedules to take time off to attend some program events and go to doctor appointments, they are not financially secure enough to have only one parent working. They don't qualify for child-care assistance or the Head Start program, and the boys' tuition is $30,000, which equates to $1,250 per month for each child. The family is fortunate that they can afford this child care, which is of about average quality. However, Regina thinks about her sister, Janice, a single mom with two children ages two and three, who does qualify for child-care assistance. In spite of this support, Janice still struggles with paying her portion of the child-care fee of about $800 per month for the two children. She often finds herself behind on her child-care fees, even though she works full-time as the administrative coordinator for a major IT firm.

Child-care assistance is made possible through the Child Care and Development Block Grant (CCDBG) enacted through the Child Care and Development Fund. The purpose of CCDBG legislation is to provide affordable child care for low-income working parents and to improve the quality of child care. According to the Pew Research Center, many households include families in which all adults in the home work.

The CCDBG focuses on making high-quality child care accessible for families who need to work. In the 1960s, 25 percent of both parents in households with children were in the labor force; this number jumped by 35 percent in 2012 to 60 percent. Early care and education is intended not only to provide a safe and enriching environment for children so they start life well, but also to provide a way for parents to work and provide economic security and stability for the family. Early care and education is a source of income for providers as well as an economic driver for communities providing care (Conti and Heckman, n.d.).

Figure 1.1. Rise in Dual Income Households

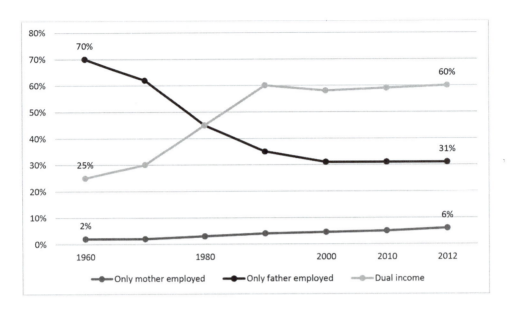

Source: Pew Research Center. 2015. Rise in Dual Income Households.
https://www.pewresearch.org/ft_dual-income-households-1960-2012-2/

This need for accessible, high-quality programs for children from poor working families has resulted in more states investing in early learning quality initiatives. In 2011, the US Departments of Education and Health and Human Services launched the $500 million Race to the Top–Early Learning Challenge grant (RTT-ELC). Many of you reading this book may have heard about this grant either through accessing professional development or working with your state's quality rating system, child-care referral agency, and other organizations. The RTT-ELC rewarded state plans that committed to building coordinated systems, aligning resources and policies, and increasing access to high-quality early learning and development programs for children who need them most. Specifically, the RTT-ELC focused on ensuring the following:

> State early childhood systems were aligned from birth through grade 3

> A common quality rating and improvement system to evaluate and improve program performance

> Common early learning standards to support child outcomes, including behavioral and health needs and family engagement

> A capable, supported, and well-compensated workforce

> Effective systems to measure outcomes and monitor progress prior to and after school entry

As we examine the RTT-ELC grant program through a social justice lens, we see the following:

1. Activation, alignment, coordination, and accountability of various systems to support the learning of children with the greatest needs

2. Valuing the role of families

3. Recognizing the importance of noncognitive skills, such as socio-emotional and self-regulation

4. Addressing inequities in the system, including skills and compensation of the workforce

5. Ensuring that learning standards meet the needs of all children

The RTT-ELC program moved from the basic notion that child care should only provide a safe and healthy place for children to be while parents are working to one that is more intentional about providing warm and enriching settings for children's holistic development. This means that the expectations for early childhood education teachers and providers, as well as directors, have shifted over time to focus on teaching credentials, professional development, learning standards, curriculum, engagement of families and communities, and addressing children's special and unique needs. From a fiscal point of view, this means that even if Regina and her husband are paying $1,250 per month per child and Janice Smith, her sister, is paying $400 per month per child, all their children should experience high-quality early education. In addition, their children should be able to get the most out of these programs. However, that is not the case when they are being suspended or excluded from a school or program.

PRESCHOOL SUSPENSION AND EXPULSION

In the mid-1990s, the Centers for Disease Control (CDC) and Kaiser Permanente conducted a study to investigate the impact that childhood trauma and neglect and household challenges have on later-life health and well-being. They found that early adversity has lasting impacts, and some populations are more vulnerable to adverse experiences because of the social and economic conditions in which they live (Felitti et al., 1998). The Adverse Childhood Experiences (ACEs) quiz below lists a number of adverse experiences (Sacks, Murphey, and Moore, 2014). Mark an X next to the ones you experienced as a child.

1. Lived with a parent or guardian who got divorced or separated

2. Lived with a parent or guardian who died

3. Lived with a parent or guardian who served time in jail or prison

4. Lived with anyone who was mentally ill or suicidal, or severely depressed for more than a couple of weeks

5. Lived with anyone who had a problem with alcohol or drugs

6. Witnessed a parent, guardian, or other adult in the household behaving violently toward another (such as slapping, hitting, kicking, punching, or beating each other up)

7. Was ever the victim of violence or witnessed any violence in my neighborhood

8. Experienced economic hardship somewhat often or very often (for example, the family found it hard to cover costs of food and housing)

9. Treated unfairly due to my race, ethnicity, language, or religion

Trauma-informed care: recognition of the pervasiveness of trauma and a commitment to identify and address it early (Hodas, 2006)

Research indicates that children who experience four or more ACEs are likely to have significant health challenges in life, including heart disease, diabetes, autoimmune abnormalities, and many more. Imagine if you could avoid these health challenges with positive experiences in the early years. Imagine if the children you teach and care for could avoid these types of traumatic early life experiences.

Reflection Questions

Please review and work on these questions during personal time in a private location. Your answers are not intended to be shared unless you want to do so.

> How many ACEs did you experience growing up?

> Have you shared this experience with others? If so, why or why not?

> How do you think that your experiences are reflected in why you are in the early education profession?

> How do you think the ACEs you experienced affect your daily life, such as your relationship with your partner, friends, and family?

> Do these experiences affect how you teach and what you teach? Do they affect how you may respond to some children?

> Do you know the ACEs scores of children in your classroom? Could this information change how you see and interact with them? Why or why not?

> What if a child's ACEs score was due, in part, to experiences with you, such as how you don't acknowledge the child or limit conversation to giving the child instructions? Would you change your approach with that child? Why or why not?

Children who experience adversities require educators who use a trauma-informed approach that considers children's individualized needs. This means that teachers have to use an *equity* approach rather than an *equality* approach in how they interact with and teach children. In most instances, teachers are focused on every child getting equal time, so no child feels neglected, excluded, or left out. An equity approach in teaching means that teachers provide children with what they need to thrive. For example, John is a four-and-a-half-year-old who lives in a two-bedroom

Equality: everyone gets the same thing regardless of their needs

Equity: everyone gets a fair and just opportunity to thrive, according to their needs (Braveman et al., 2017)

apartment with his two parents, granddad, and three siblings. At least once a week he is kept awake by the sirens from either ambulances or police cars. He has told his teacher that he loves the waterworks area. The teacher has learned that his parents often take their children to the aquarium, and John has told his parents the ocean and water calm him down and help him sleep because he thinks about the fish.

Typically, the waterworks area is available to the children in John's classroom for 20 minutes at a time. Given that John feels soothed and calm in the waterworks station and often wants to remain there beyond the allotted 20 minutes, why not give him an extra 15 minutes and let him stay for a total of 35 minutes? The equal approach would be to demand that he leave the waterworks area after 20 minutes because of the rule. In contrast, the equitable approach is to consider those 15 minutes of soothing time as a way to help John regulate so that he is able to engage in the next lesson and experience. Similarly, another child may need an extra hug, pat on the back, and even a one-on-one activity with the assistant teacher. The value is in recognizing that, depending on children's context and experience, there may be a need to change one's behaviors to support each child in a way to help her thrive.

As we will discuss in chapter 2, educators often don't realize the impact of White privilege and institutional racism on the learning experiences and opportunities of Black children and other children of color. This means that we often focus on ensuring that all children have the same or equal experiences and opportunities without recognizing that, in doing so, we are maintaining an inequitable system. In this system, White children are already privileged, and Black children and other children of color are playing catch-up from the start due to discrimination, bias, and the legacy of racism.

> We often focus on ensuring that all children have the same or equal experiences and opportunities without recognizing that, in doing so, we are maintaining an inequitable system.

For example, some children prefer written storytelling, and others prefer oral storytelling. Educators prefer and privilege book reading that is sequential and goes from main idea to ending. However, Black children in particular favor oral storytelling that is context driven, meaning that a story about their night may pull in other contexts, such as a time at the park or going to visit Grandma, and it is not sequential. Rather than focusing on the richness of the story and language, teachers often focus on the lack of sequence that is more common with a White, Eurocentric approach to stories (Gardner-Neblett, Pungello, and Iruka, 2012). This is why it is critical to provide different learning modalities and opportunities for children to better meet their needs.

DON'T LOOK AWAY: EMBRACING ANTI-BIAS CLASSROOMS

CHAPTER 2:

WHITE PRIVILEGE AND INSTITUTIONAL RACISM

This chapter will discuss institutional racism and White privilege and how they affect the experiences and outcomes of children of color in early childhood. We will examine the role of educators as the first social-justice teachers to potentially begin to dismantle the impacts of racism and inequities on children and families.

> *What that conversation is about is when a community has been left behind for generations because of the color of their skin. When you've been denied job after job after job because you're Black or because you're brown. So institutional racism is real. It doesn't take away your pain or suffering. It's just a different issue. Your suffering is just as important as a Black or brown person's suffering, but to fix the problems that are happening in a Black community, you need far more transformational efforts that are targeted for real racism that exists every day.*
>
> *—Senator Kirsten Gillibrand of New York responding to a person who asked, "What do you have to say to people in this area [Ohio] about so-called White privilege?"*

According to the US Census Bureau, babies of color now outnumber non-Hispanic White babies (Cohn, 2016). On July 1, 2015, the population of racial or ethnic minority babies was 50.2 percent of the total population of the United States. This means that out of ten babies born, five of them likely are non-White. Even if you are not a demographer who studies population change, you can imagine that if this pattern continues for twenty-five years, you are likely to see a big shift in the demographic make-up of the United States. This shift in demographics is supported by the US Department of Education data shown in Figure 2.1, which indicates that children of color now make up the majority of public-school students enrolled in prekindergarten through twelfth grade, and that this number will rise by 2025. This means that children of color are the majority, and this majority will continue to increase.

There has also been a slight increase in the number of dual language learners (DLLs) and English Language Learners (ELLs) who make up school enrollment. DLLs and ELLs make up about 9 percent of the public-school population, meaning that for every ten students, at least one of them speaks a language other than English or is learning English (Musu-Gillette et al., 2016). For some sites, this may be a much larger percentage.

Despite the fact that children of color are now the majority, this has not resulted in changes in their experiences. For example, according to the Pew Research Center, the teaching workforce does not look like them (Geiger, 2018). Often, books and curricula don't accurately reflect their cultures or communities. There are children who don't feel that they belong. They don't have the power their numerical majority suggests, meaning that they are still treated like lower-class citizens.

Figure 2.1

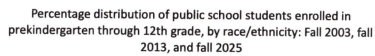

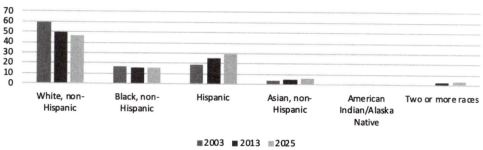

Source: U.S. Department of Education, National Center for Education Statistics, Common Core of Data (CCD), "State Nonfiscal Survey of Public Elementary and Secondary Education," 2003–04 and 2013–14; and National Elementary and Secondary Enrollment Projection Model, 1972 through 2025. See Digest of Education Statistics 2015, table 203.50.

WHITE PRIVILEGE
AND INSTITUTIONAL RACISM

White privilege is a set of advantages and immunities that White people, because they are the dominant power group, benefit from on a daily basis. Black people and other people of color do not benefit from this set of advantages and immunities. White privilege assumes that people who are White are more valuable than non-

White people. For example, as explained by Senator Gillibrand to a woman in Youngstown, Ohio:

> So, if your son is fifteen years old and smokes pot. He smokes pot just as much as a Black boy in his neighborhood and the Latino boy in his neighborhood. But that Black and brown boy is [sic] four times more likely to get arrested. And when he's arrested, that criminal justice system might require him to pay bail: 500 bucks. That kid does not have 500 bucks. He might not be able to make bail. As an adult with a child at home—he's a single parent—if he is thrown in jail, no one is with his child. It doesn't matter what he says, "I have to go home. I have a child at home, he's only twelve. What am I going to do?" It doesn't matter. Imagine as a parent how you would feel so helpless. That's institutional racism. Your son will likely not have to deal with that because he is White. So, when someone says White privilege, that is all they are talking about—that his Whiteness will mean that a police officer might give him a second chance. It might mean that he doesn't get incarcerated because he has just smoked a joint with his girlfriend. It might mean that he won't have to post bail. It means he might be able to show up to work the next day and not lose his job and not be in the cycle of poverty that never ends.

White privilege means that a White male who has committed a crime is given the benefit of the doubt: he is from a good family, meant no harm, and deserves a second chance. His life means more than that of a Black male, who is viewed as less-than and incapable. Unfortunately, Black children are often not given the benefit of the doubt. Coupled with these biases are the structural racism and inequities that punish Black children and other children of color more harshly than White children.

Reflection Question

Have you given a "pass" to a White child because you believed the child had made a one-time mistake and would do great things when he got older?

Three-Strikes Laws

President Bill Clinton signed into law the Violent Crime Control and Law Enforcement Act of 1994, which contains a so-called "three-strikes" provision mandating life imprisonment without possibility of parole for federal offenders with three or more convictions for serious violent felonies or drug-trafficking crimes (18 U.S.C. § 3559(c)). Several states have laws requiring at least a twenty-five-year sentence for offenders convicted of a violent crime in addition to being convicted of two previous violent crimes (such as rape, murder, or armed robbery) or serious crimes (such as burglary of a residence or assault with intent to commit robbery). According to the *Los Angeles Times*, an analysis by the California Department of Corrections found that 85 percent of all inmates incarcerated under the state's three-strikes law were found guilty of nonviolent offenses in their second or third convictions. In application, third-strike sentences have resulted in a large proportion of Blacks being imprisoned. For example, two years after its enactment, the state of California's three-strikes sentencing law resulted in an imprisonment rate of Blacks that was thirteen times higher than that of Whites, the *Times* reports (Krikorian, 1996). Among Black men in their twenties, 39 percent were imprisoned or on probation. By comparison, the rate was about one in ten for young Latino males and one in twenty for young White males. There is no evidence that Black people commit more crimes than White people; however, the bias inherent in the United States that sees Black people and other people of color as aggressive and violent has resulted in their being overpoliced.

According to the US Census Bureau, 60.4 percent of the population is White and not Hispanic or Latinx, 13.4 percent is Black, and 18.3 percent is Hispanic or Latinx. Despite representing a smaller proportion of the population, Black people are more likely to be incarcerated and subjected to the trauma of the dehumanizing nature of prison, losing time for education, being left behind in school, dropping out, limiting employment opportunities because of a criminal record and race, and potentially becoming lifelong criminals and prisoners.

There have been many instances of Black people and other people of color doing ordinary activities that caused them to be policed without cause. Consider the following:

> Rashon Nelson and Donte Robinson waited in a Philadelphia Starbucks on April 12, 2018, to meet with a business partner. After waiting less than 10 minutes, they were surrounded by police, arrested, and faced charges for trespassing and creating a disturbance.

> In May 2018, Lolade Siyonbola, a Black graduate student at Yale University, woke from a nap in a common room in her dormitory to questions from police. A classmate had called 911, saying that she wasn't sure if Siyonbola belonged in the dorm.

> On June 14, 2018, Mia Irizarry visited an Illinois park to set up for her birthday party in an area she had rented for the celebration. There, she was berated by a man because she was wearing a shirt with a Puerto Rican flag on it. The man taunted her by saying her shirt was "un-American." His taunting happened while a police officer stood by and did not intervene, even when Irizarry told the officer she felt unsafe and asked for his help. More police officers were called to the scene, and they asked Irizarry for an ID when they arrived, prompting the police to issue a statement about tolerance. (The man who berated her was eventually arrested and charged with hate crimes, assault, and disorderly conduct.)

> A White neighbor called the police on a twelve-year-old Ohio boy operating a mowing business and said he was cutting the wrong lawn.

> A White man in Winston-Salem, North Carolina, called the police on a Black woman and her son for using the neighborhood pool; this man lost his job.

> In June 2018, a White woman called 911 on an eight-year-old Black girl selling water in San Francisco, arguing that the girl's mother was being too loud and that they were illegally selling water.

> In May 2018, Aaron Schlossberg, a New York attorney, was caught on tape yelling at the employees of a Fresh Kitchen restaurant in Manhattan, berating them for speaking Spanish to customers. He said, "My guess is they're not documented, so my next call is to ICE to have each one of them kicked out of my country. They have the balls to come here and live off of my money; I pay for their welfare; I pay for their ability to be here. The least they could do, the least they could do is speak English."

As stated in a national news outlet, "These aren't the only incidents. Be it a Black firefighter doing safety inspections in a largely White neighborhood, Black teens shopping at a Nordstrom Rack in Missouri, a Black family holding a barbecue, a different Black family eating, or a Black real estate investor looking at a property, people of color are repeatedly racially profiled, confronted by police, and, in some cases, arrested after White business owners, employees, or bystanders viewed them with suspicion" (Lockhart, 2018). These incidents are visited on Black people and other people of color while engaging in ordinary activities. ==White people, on the other hand, do not need to fear that the police will be called on them when they are engaged in everyday activities.==

Fortunately, the incidents described did not result in death; however, there are many in which the perception of Black people and people of color as violent and threatening did result in death. Thus, while some may believe that biases are just people "behaving badly" or being disrespectful, there are many instances that have led to serious—even deadly—consequences.

> Eric Garner, 43, died on July 17, 2014, after being confronted by police on Staten Island, New York, for allegedly selling cigarettes illegally. Garner raised both hands in the air and told the officers not to touch him, but the officer put him in a choke hold and while he screamed, "I can't breathe! I can't breathe!"

> Freddie Gray, 25, died in custody after being injured in a Baltimore, Maryland, police van, an incident that led to multiday riots in the city.

> Philando Castile, 32, a Black motorist in Falcon Heights, Minnesota, informed an officer during a traffic stop that he was carrying a legal gun for which he had a permit. When he reached for the permit, after telling the officer that he wasn't reaching for a weapon, he was shot to death. Castile's girlfriend streamed the aftermath live on Facebook, showing their preschool-age child running from the car as Castile is fatally shot. Fortunately, an officer picked up and embraced the child and carried her away from the scene.

> Terence Crutcher, 40, was shot in Tulsa, Oklahoma, shortly after officer Betty Jo Shelby arrived to find Crutcher's SUV stopped in the middle of the road. Shelby testified that she was afraid of Crutcher because he did not obey her commands and seemed to reach into his vehicle. The video footage, however, shows him walking away from the officers toward his vehicle with his hands over his head. He is tasered, then shot.

> Alton Sterling, 37, was shot to death on July 5, 2016, in Baton Rouge, Louisiana, as officers pinned him to the pavement outside a convenience store where he had been selling CDs.

> Tamir Rice, 12, was fatally shot by a White police officer in Cleveland, Ohio. The officer had responded to a call that a person in a park, possibly a juvenile, was waving a gun and pointing it at people. Officers confused the pellet gun that Tamir was playing with with a real weapon.

> Antwon Rose II, 17, was shot by East Pittsburgh, Pennsylvania, police officer Michael Rosfeld while riding in a car with friends. Police suspected that the occupants in the

car were involved in a drive-by shooting. Antwon was an unarmed passenger in the car (Associated Press, 2017; NewsOne, 2019).

These incidents are a reminder about how the lives of Black people and other people of color have always been devalued throughout this country's history. Not only are these men dead, but also the trauma visited on their partners, children, families, and communities continues long after their deaths.

INSTITUTIONAL RACISM AND THE IMPACT ON BLACK LIVES

Blacks are a unique subpopulation in US history, because they are the only group that has ever been deemed as "property" that could be bought, sold, and dispensed with without any legal consequence. In fact, the law actually condoned and supported these practices for more than 250 years. This is called *institutional* or *structural racism*—when laws and policies are enacted to support inequities and unequal treatment, ensuring that the majority power group—White people, in the United States—are privileged and remain in power. During centuries in which Blacks were regarded as property, society's view of them changed to justify the system of commerce that was dependent upon their free labor. Blacks were viewed as nonhumans, unentitled to any legal rights or liberties. Unfortunately, even after hundreds of years of slavery, Blacks were subjected to another eighty-eight years of Jim Crow laws. These laws were essentially a caste system that permitted the government and members of society to treat Blacks as second-class citizens who were granted only limited rights and protection under the law. This legal structure led to Blacks being less likely than Whites to own homes and acquire wealth; less likely to attend high-quality schools; less likely to find employment; if employed, less likely to earn fair and equitable wages; and to their being more likely to be incarcerated. It has only been in the last fifty-four years that American Blacks have been granted their full legal and societal rights as human beings. This long history of repression and abuse in the United States provides a sobering foundation for the current lives of African Americans. It is the reason why people wonder whether Black lives matter as much as others'—when for centuries it was clear that their lives did not matter at all.

This long history still has negative ramifications today. Often, racial oppression or bias manifests in the form of daily unconscious biases and microaggressions experienced by Black children. Our unconscious biases are represented by our thoughts, feelings, and values that guide our daily decision-making, even when we are unaware of such thoughts, feelings, or values. Microaggressions are the "constant and continuing reality of slights, insults, invalidations, and indignities visited upon marginalized groups by sometimes well-intentioned, moral, and decent family members, friends, neighbors, coworkers, students, teachers, clerks, waiters and waitresses, employers, health care professionals and educators" (Wing Sue, 2010; Portman, Bui, Ogaz, and Treviño, n.d.). Some examples of microaggression include the following:

> Mispronouncing certain children's names, even after multiple corrections, because they are not traditionally "White" names

> Assuming a Hispanic child speaks Spanish or is undocumented

> Asking Black students in a class whether their family will have chicken and watermelon at dinner

> Calling on one group of children and ignoring others based on gender, race, and/or class

> Assigning roles based on gender, race, and/or class, such as assigning White girls to play in the library center or pretend to be teachers and assigning Black children to play in the cleaning and housekeeping center

We know from decades of data that many people see Black people as "less than," "lazy," "shiftless," "criminals," "unintelligent," and so forth (Blake, 2017). This perception about non-White people, especially Blacks, is deeply rooted within all sectors of our society and, therefore, has an impact on how everyone, including early education professionals, behaves. Bias affects a person's viewpoint and, subsequently, how a person interacts with Black children and other children of color. Can you imagine your daughter, son, grandchild, niece, or nephew being viewed and treated as less than, even before they can talk? Or maybe you are a

Microaggressions: the constant and continuing reality of slights, insults, invalidations, and indignities visited upon marginalized groups

person of color, and you or a loved one has experienced the suspicious stares, racial profiling, or microaggressions.

Reflection Questions

> How many children are in your classroom or program?

> How many of those children are non-White? How many are Black? How many are Hispanic? How many speak a language other than English?

> Have you seen a change in the population of children in your classroom or program? If so, why do you think that is?

> How do you think this change, if any, affects your teaching or the classroom culture? For example, do you have more small-group activities or choice time or more whole-group instruction and routines? Do you see children with better language or behavior, or the opposite? Do you see more family engagement or less?

WHAT DO THE CHANGING DEMOGRAPHICS MEAN FOR EARLY CHILDHOOD PROFESSIONALS?

The changing demographics can be challenging for some early childhood professionals who have been accustomed to primarily teaching White children. What does it mean if the children in your programs are immigrants, speak a language other than English, or are being raised by a grandparent? It may require a little bit more effort to understand children's early learning experiences, learn how to effectively communicate with children and families, or understand how best to support a child being raised by a relative or nonbiological parent due to incarceration or immigration policies that may result in families being separated. There is evidence that, due to the vestiges of racism and discrimination that tore families apart through slavery, lynching, incarceration, drugs, or death, Black children are more likely than White children to live in single-parent households or with grandparents or nonbiological parents such as foster parents (US Census Bureau, 2015). This change in demographics should not reduce the quality of teaching, but it may mean that more attention should be paid to the experiences and needs of individual children, especially those who may be experiencing challenges such as the loss of a parent, learning a new language, or recent immigration, especially when the policies are unfairly targeting and punishing them because of their color, race, or ethnicity. This may mean there are other areas in their lives that may be a challenge, such as securing safe and stable housing and health access. Unfortunately, studies have shown that children of color and children from low-income households are likely to have low-quality experiences, including in their early childhood classrooms.

HOW RACE AND PROGRAM QUALITY INTERSECT

Can a child's race really determine the quality of his early learning program?

The majority of early childhood educators would say that they are in this profession because they love children and want the best for all the children in their care. However, this motivation does not always translate to what children actually experience. In a national study from the US Department of Education, researchers found that the year before kindergarten, 65 percent of four-year-old children were likely to be in low-to-moderate-quality center-based programs (see Figure 2.2) (Barnett, Carolan, and Johns, 2013). This means that many center-based programs engaged in few enriching interactions with children and provided minimal learning materials that don't effectively support children's learning. This number of four-year-old children in low-to-moderate-quality programs jumped to 91 percent for home-based programs. This is a form of institutional racism. We should be providing equal quality care to all children, but we are instead disproportionately providing lower-quality care, especially to children who need it the most.

Figure 2.2. Percentage Distribution of Quality Rating of Child-Care Arrangements of Children at about 4 Years of Age, by Type of Arrangement and Race/Ethnicity: 2005–06

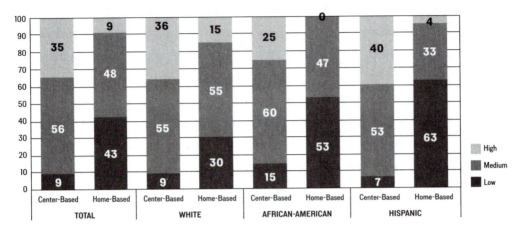

Source: U.S. Department of Education, National Center for Education Statistics, Early Childhood Longitudinal Study, Birth Cohort 9-month–Kindergarten Restricted-Use Date File and Electronic Codebook. Table 57. (December 2010)

When we look at these numbers by racial groups, we see that 60 percent of Hispanic children, 64 percent of White children, and 75 percent of Black children are in low-to-moderate-quality center-based programs. When we look at home-based programs, we see that 85 percent of White children, 96 percent of Hispanic children, and 100 percent of Black children are in low-to-moderate-quality programs. It is absolutely astounding that so many children are likely to experience poor-to-average-quality programs in the year before they start kindergarten. For Black and Latinx or Hispanic children, who are often starting out behind their White peers, it is even more staggering that all children in home-based programs are likely to be in low-to-average-quality programs. Consider these numbers in light of the fact that 68 percent of Black children under the age of five are in child care, compared to 62 percent of White children and 51 percent of Latinx children (Musu-Gillette et al., 2016). As an important institution, early care and education is supposed to ensure that all children start off well and on a trajectory of success in school and life.

HOW RACE AND ACEs INTERSECT

Many children, especially Black children, may not be experiencing the promise of early education, even in programs of low-to-moderate quality. This is evident in the preschool suspension and expulsion data from the US Department of Education, Office of Civil Rights (see Figure 2.3). In its 2013–2014 Civil Rights Data Collection, the Department of Education found that Black public preschool children are 3.6 times more likely than their White counterparts to receive one or more out-of-school suspensions. Black children represent only 18 percent of preschool enrollment, but 48 percent of preschool children who receive one or more out-of-school suspensions; in comparison, White children represent 41 percent of preschool enrollment, but 28 percent of those receiving one or more out-of-school suspensions. For example, imagine one preschool program with 100 children, of whom forty-three are White, twenty-nine are Hispanic, eighteen Black, four Asian, two American Indian, and four biracial/multiracial. If this program reported the number of children who were suspended more than once, you would assume about the same number across racial groups. For example, if there were 100 suspensions, we would expect that White children would make up about 43 percent of multiple suspensions, Hispanic children 29 percent, and Black children 18 percent of cases. Based on real data, however, this is not the case. White children make up 26 percent of multiple suspension rates, which is 17 percent lower than their population. Hispanic children make up 20 percent of multiple suspension rates, which is 9 percent lower than their population rate. But for Black children, who comprise only 18 percent of the population, the multiple suspension rate is 48 percent—30 percent above their population rate! This means that for every two multiple suspensions in preschool, Black children make up one of those suspensions. Layer these findings with the information showing that Black children are likely to be in lower-quality prekindergarten programs compared to their peers.

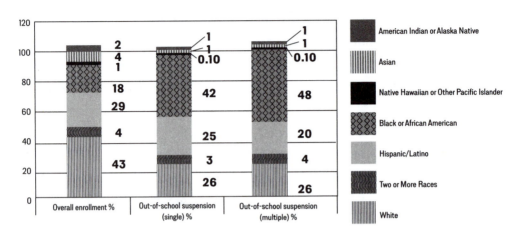

Figure 2.3. Preschool Expulsion and Suspension Rates by Race and Ethnicity

Source. Office for Civil Rights. (2014). Data Snapshot: School Discipline, Issue Brief No. 1. Washington, DC: U.S. Department of Education, Office for Civil Rights

Could it be that Black children are really misbehaving more than their peers and thus need to be suspended? Or is there something else at work? Early educators indicate that the main reasons for suspensions include fighting, not listening, misbehaving, not sitting still, being disrespectful, and being viewed as a danger to themselves or others (Skiba, Michael, Nardo, and Peterson, 2002; Gilliam and Reyes, 2018). Most educators indicate that they use suspension and expulsion as a last-ditch effort to minimize the impact of a child's disruptive or unsafe behaviors on other children. Children growing up in challenging circumstances, such as domestic abuse, poverty, and neighborhood violence, are at greater risk of having socio-emotional, cognitive, and behavioral challenges, any of which can negatively impact their attention and self-regulation. There is more evidence coming out about the lifetime impact on adverse childhood experiences (ACEs). We are learning that ACEs affect children's functioning, including their brain development; their regulation skills, such as being able to sit still and pay attention; and their ability to learn. This means that children who have witnessed their parents being arrested or killed, who hear gunshots in their neighborhoods, or who live in homes where they witness domestic violence or substance abuse are likely to show problematic behaviors, if untreated. While children growing up in poor households are likely to experience more ACEs than those in middle-income and higher-income households, ACEs are seen in all types of households across all ethnic groups. Nevertheless, there is some indication that

ACE-adverse childhood experiences

children of color are likely to experience more ACEs and poverty compared to White children. In Figure 2.4, we see that 15 percent of Black children, compared to 11 percent of White and Hispanic children, were likely to experience three or more ACEs.

Figure 2.4. Percentage of children with different levels of adverse experience by race and Hispanic origin

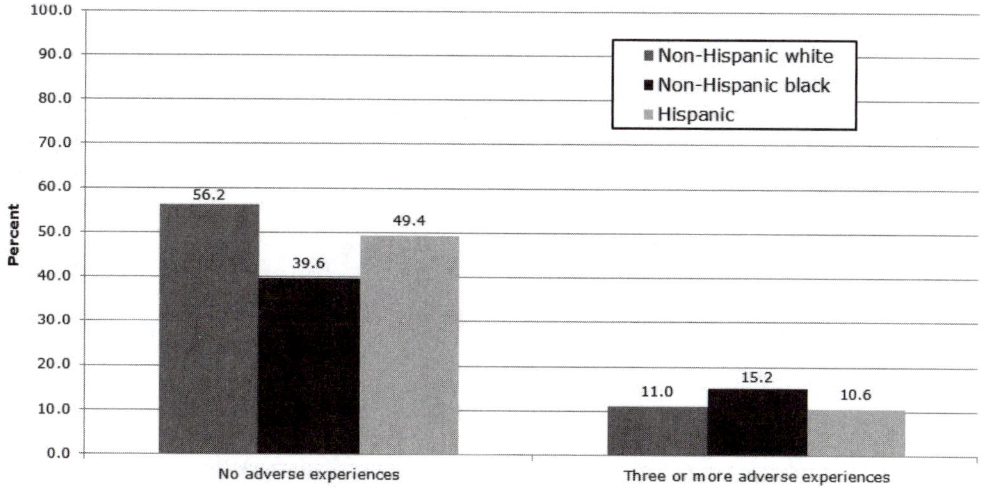

Source: Child Trends' original analyses of data from the National Survey of Children's Health.

Even in regions of the country, such as the Mountain or West North Central areas, where there are low minority populations, children of color are likely to have more ACEs than White children (see Figure 2.5).

Figure 2.5. Percentage of children with one adverse childhood experience by region

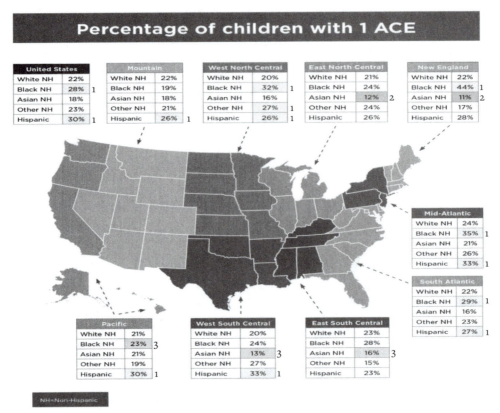

Percentage of children with 1 ACE

United States		
White NH	22%	
Black NH	28%	1
Asian NH	18%	
Other NH	23%	
Hispanic	30%	1

Mountain		
White NH	22%	
Black NH	19%	
Asian NH	18%	
Other NH	21%	
Hispanic	26%	1

West North Central		
White NH	20%	
Black NH	32%	1
Asian NH	16%	
Other NH	27%	1
Hispanic	26%	1

East North Central		
White NH	21%	
Black NH	24%	
Asian NH	12%	2
Other NH	24%	
Hispanic	26%	

New England		
White NH	22%	
Black NH	44%	1
Asian NH	11%	2
Other NH	17%	
Hispanic	28%	

Mid-Atlantic	
White NH	24%
Black NH	35% 1
Asian NH	21%
Other NH	26%
Hispanic	33% 1

South Atlantic	
White NH	22%
Black NH	29% 1
Asian NH	16%
Other NH	23%
Hispanic	27% 1

Pacific		
White NH	21%	
Black NH	23%	3
Asian NH	21%	
Other NH	19%	
Hispanic	30%	1

West South Central		
White NH	20%	
Black NH	24%	
Asian NH	13%	3
Other NH	27%	
Hispanic	33%	1

East South Central		
White NH	23%	
Black NH	28%	
Asian NH	16%	3
Other NH	15%	
Hispanic	23%	

NH=Non-Hispanic

1 = Percentage is higher than White non-Hispanic children at a statistically significant level

2 = Percentage is lower than White non-Hispanic children at a statistically significant level

3 = Estimate should be interpreted with caution because the relative confidence interval is greater than 120 percent.

While ACEs are not a problem confined to those in poverty, studies indicate that poverty can increase stressors such as domestic violence and drug and alcohol abuse among caregivers, which lead to trauma and could have implications for children's emotional development. Black children and other children of color are more likely to live in poor and violent communities compared to their White peers. More than six out of ten children of color are from low-income households (see Figure 2.6). Black and Latinx families are likely to live in segregated areas, which could be unsafe and violent.

Imagine being a child who lives in a neighborhood where there are not many streetlights, but where you often hear car horns and "popping" noises several nights a week. You stay up at night until you hear your father walk into the house.

Not only are children of color, especially Black children, more likely than White children to come from low-income families, they are also more likely to reside in segregated poor communities with a lack of quality child care, health services, and readily available nutritious food. Lack of adequate sleep, food, and shelter can cause children to live in a state of hypersensitivity and arousal, limiting their ability to focus and attend (NASEM, 2019). A child who has not had enough to eat can only think about food rather than be engaged in the lesson of the day. Similarly, a child with limited or no sleep would have low energy to concentrate and engage and would likely be more irritable. Thus, the environments children experience inside and outside their early education programs have an impact on their ability to regulate and attend.

We have seen what living in poor communities can mean for one's health and well-being when we think of the Flint, Michigan, water crisis, which largely impacted poor and mostly Black families. We have the imagery of a tale of two cities. On one side, "the good side," is a bustling area with lot of things happening, such as fairs, parades, stores, bars, restaurants, families outside walking their dogs, and neighbors shouting hello across the street. Then there is the other side of the city, "the bad side," that has dim lights where there is an eerie silence with no stores except a gas station that closes at 6:30 p.m. Which side of the city would you like to live on? Which side of town would you want your children to go to school in? What if you could afford to live on only "the bad side" of town? Are you a teacher from the good side teaching on the bad side or teaching children from the bad side of town? Are you a teacher from the bad side teaching children from the good or from the bad side? Do you see children from the good side and children from the bad side differently?

Figure 2.6. Percentage of Children in Low Income and Poor Families by Race/Ethnicity

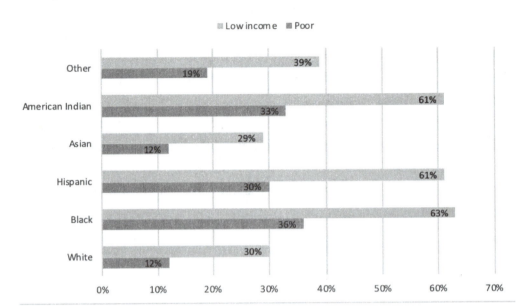

(Jian, Granja, and Koball, 2017)

Let us return to the scenario of whether Black children are misbehaving more than their peers. Behavior is likely to be influenced by all the circumstances described—and more. The stressors that Black children may experience throughout their lives could lead to poor self-regulation. The racism and bias often visited upon Black children could compound the issue by assuming that Black children are often misbehaving rather than simply being children. As early educators, we must understand children's contexts and experiences. There is no indication that trauma targets children by race; rather, adults traumatize children in many ways, which can affect them throughout their schooling and lives.

HOW RACE AND OPPORTUNITY INTERSECT

According to researchers at the Brookings Institution, a nonprofit public-policy organization, there is a 30 percent chance that a child from a low-income family will make it into the middle class as an adult (see Figure 2.7). So a child born in poverty is likely to remain in poverty; this is especially the case for Black children and other children of color. The area you live in determines your schooling experience, which then links to whether or not and where you go to college, which can determine the kind of work you do and the life experiences you have, which then shapes your adult life. For those who may have many obstacles from birth throughout adulthood, the chances of a successful transition from childhood through adulthood are low. There are many bumps along the way compared to someone who had privileges due to their wealth, race, and gender (Sawhill, Winship, and Grannis, 2012).

Figure 2.7. Success Rates at Each Life Stage, by Family Income

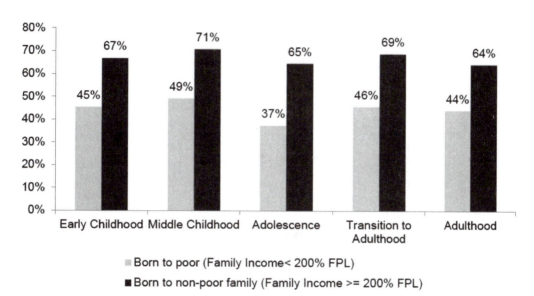

Source: Sawhill, I. V., & Karpilow, 2014. *How much could we improve children's life chances by intervening early and often*, CCF Brief #54. Washington, DC: Center on Children and Families at Brookings.

If there is only a 30 percent chance that a person born in poverty is going to successfully make it into at least the middle class as an adult, what does it mean for children of color who are likely to be poor? What does it mean as we become a "majority minority" country? If more of our citizenry are poor as children, and they will remain poor as adults, then this has implications for our country. For example, this means that many of the children will not be able to take on the jobs that we need. They won't have enough money to contribute to Social Security or Medicare or even pay enough taxes to help cities take care of roads, social safety, and education. The national debt may never be paid because of a low-income tax base. Our ability to remain a critical actor in the world may be diminished.

The learning gap between minority and White children is seen as early as nine months of age and continues to increase over time. We see a gap of more than twenty points between White and ethnic minority students through the K–12 period (see Figure 2.8). While there is some evidence that the racial gap is decreasing, the income gap is increasing. This comes at the same time that more minority children, especially Black children, have seen an increase in poverty rates.

Figure 2.8: Trend in Eighth-Grade NAEP Reading Average Scores and Score Gaps, by Selected Racial/Ethnic Groups

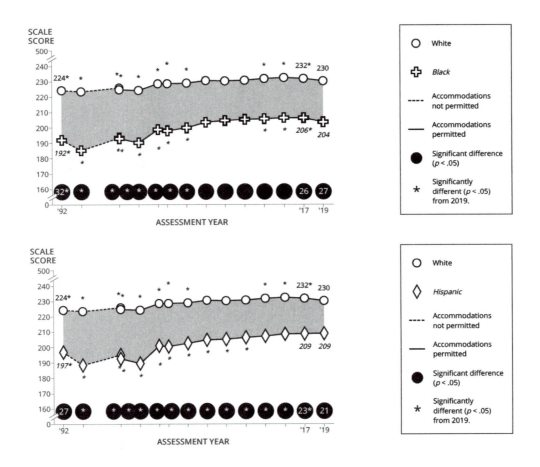

At the current rate of change, it will take at least 100 years for the racial gap to be eliminated. We can't wait that long. As early educators, we recognize that the pathway to school and life success starts in the first few years of life. Our role is to ensure that all children are at the starting line at the same time with the same resources and opportunities. We can't move children 500 feet behind the starting Aline wearing cinderblock shoes with a wall in front of them and expect them to do as well as the children at the front of the line with skates and bicycles. Some children have had a head start in life because of their race, gender, family wealth, and zip code. In contrast, others have had more challenges in life because of their race, gender, lack of wealth, and zip code. In this book, we seek to provide a lens through which to examine the potential of children who don't have privilege and access and how we can work hard to ensure they are at the starting line with the same opportunity to run the race and have the potential to win.

As early educators, we recognize that the pathway to school and life success starts in the first few years of life. Our role is to ensure that all children are at the starting line at the same time with the same resources and opportunities.

Group Activity: Privilege Walk

Note: It is important not to mention the title of this exercise before it happens. Let participants come up with their own ideas about the meaning and significance of this experience. The idea of this exercise is for people to think about the privilege they have and how others are affected when one group has privileges and others, who do not, remain marginalized from opportunities.

Facilitator: To begin, please form a straight line in the middle of the room facing the east wall. We will read a series of statements asking you to take a step backward or forward, depending on your experience with the statement. We ask that you do this exercise in silence, helping to maintain a reflective atmosphere for all participants. (Read a series of statements, allowing participants time to respond by moving either forward or backward.)

> "If you grew up with enough food to eat, take one step forward."

> "If you had your own room when you were growing up, take a step forward."

> "If you never worried about your safety when growing up, take a step forward."

> "If your family had money to buy clothes and shoes when you were growing up, take a step forward."

> "If you went on summer vacations when you were growing up, take a step forward."

You may also want to come up with your own statements pertaining to the focus of your dialogue, such as race, ethnicity, religion, or national origin.

Facilitator: Standing where you are, take a minute to look around the room. Notice where you are standing, notice where others are standing, and notice how you feel. (Pause). Everyone quietly return to your seats.

At first, it is important to focus on participants' experiences during this exercise. People will have different reactions to moving backward and forward as well as to the ending statement. The content of the statements may also elicit strong reactions from participants. After participants' experiences in the exercise are acknowledged, it is important to relate these experiences to situations in society such as the invisibility of privilege and oppression, feelings of living in poverty and disadvantage, and the feelings often associated with belonging to a particular social class. It is also important to acknowledge that we all have multiple identities, some of which are privileged and others that are not privileged, within US society.

Reflection Activity: Privilege Walk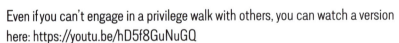

Even if you can't engage in a privilege walk with others, you can watch a version here: https://youtu.be/hD5f8GuNuGQ

Please reflect on the following.

> What is this activity about?

> What are your initial reactions/feelings about the activity?

> How do you think it would feel to take steps backward and forward?

> Have you ever thought about your place in this system? If not, why not? If yes, what have you been thinking about? Please be specific.

CHAPTER 3:

WHAT IF EDUCATORS CHANGED THE WORLD?

All students want their teachers to stand up for them, but Black and brown students need them to stand up against the rejection that suggests we have no right to be in the center of the pedagogy.

—Howard Stevenson, PhD, Constance Clayton Professor of Urban Education and Executive Director of the Racial Empowerment Collaborative at the University of Pennsylvania Graduate School of Education

We open this chapter highlighting the potentially powerful role teachers play in the educational lives of children. White teachers' power, in particular, comes from their sheer numbers; they comprise the vast majority of the educational workforce in the United States. Taie and Goldring (2017) break down teacher-workforce data across school types, and they report several important demographic trends.

> White teachers (from all genders) are 81 percent of the teacher workforce in public schools and 71 percent of the workforce in charter schools.

> Among public-school teachers, 9 percent are Hispanic, 7 percent are Black, and 2 percent are Asian.

> Among charter-school teachers, 15 percent are Hispanic, 9 percent are Black, and 3 percent are Asian.

> In our highest-poverty schools (defined as 75 percent or more students receiving free or reduced lunch), there is a higher proportion of Hispanic (16 percent) and Black (13 percent) educators; however, even in these schools, White teachers, comprising 65 percent, still far outnumber teachers of color.

Women in particular have the most influence on young children, because women (across all races and ethnicities) comprise four out of every five primary teachers. These numbers show the magnitude of White female teachers' educational influence and force us to acknowledge the sobering fact that, to change Black children's daily educational experiences, we must change the hearts and minds of White teachers. This is a hard feat to accomplish given that only 74 percent of teachers of all races report receiving any preservice education related to cultural competence (National Voices Project, 2016) and only 64 percent report receiving preservice education related to teaching children from diverse socioeconomic backgrounds (Taie and Goldring, 2017).

Another reason why this is a hard feat is because the American education system was intentionally created to legally exclude Black children from public education. From 1635, when the Boston Latin School was opened, until 1852, when Massachusetts made public school compulsory, the United States was operating under a racial caste system based on the enslavement of Americans of African descent. This caste system legally excluded enslaved Africans and their descendants from being educated in any formal school or being taught to read. In 1865, the 13th Amendment to the US Constitution abolished slavery; the 14th Amendment in 1868 granted legal

de facto - in fact, whether by right or not

citizenship status to any person born or naturalized in the United States, including Blacks who had been enslaved. Yet, Blacks' legal rights to a free public education were still limited due to the system of Jim Crow segregation in the South that existed from the late 1870s until 1954 with the US Supreme Court decision of Brown v. Board of Education of Topeka, Kansas. Although the South operated based on legal segregation (*de jure* segregation), the rest of America operated (and still does operate) based on *de facto* segregation—a tradition of racial segregation that exists even without legality.

Even today, many Black children are still educated in racially and economically segregated school systems throughout the country. The majority of Black children are being taught in a *de facto* segregated system by teachers who are culturally different from them and, often, ill-prepared to teach them. With such an imbalance of power, how could we expect the Black children to succeed?

But what if we could help teachers, particularly White teachers, to harness their power in a way that edifies, protects, and empowers children of color? We propose that teachers accomplish that goal by doing the following things:

> Conduct an authentic self-inventory of their own cultural awareness and racial biases by using tools such as the Cultural Awareness Inventory (Boehman, 1987), available at http://www.myacpa.org/sites/default/files/q%26s.pdf

   Directions: Attitudes affect behavior. To better understand how your present attitudes toward cultural differences affect your relationships with others, please respond yes or no to the statements, whichever most accurately describes your feelings.

   1. Only schools with racial problems should be concerned about racial or multicultural issues.

   2. You need to be a minority person to really understand minority issues.

   3. Color is unimportant—nobody cares about race anymore.

   4. White people cannot be trusted.

   5. Blacks are always using race to gain an advantage.

   6. Basically, there are people on this staff (who need training on multicultural issues) who would not attend this in-service if given the choice.

7. Black males are more likely to challenge the authority of staff and administration.

8. White students have few discipline problems.

9. If an Asian student is enrolled in my class, I don't have a chance of making a high grade in this course.

10. Asian students are taking away the privileges White students should have.

11. When I see a White man with a Black lady, I get angry.

12. When I see a Black man with a White lady, I feel mad. Who does he think he is anyway?

13. My friends would put me down if I started hanging out with Black people.

14. White people are always changing the rules to their advantage.

15. If given a choice, I would refuse to be roommates with a person who was not of my culture.

> Challenge their misperceptions.
> Work to diversify the field.

UNDERSTANDING RACIAL BIAS

Racism is a long-term systemic structural problem in society that is manifested not only through interpersonal actions, such as microaggressions, hate crimes, and racial slurs, but also through institutional practices and societal laws, such as slavery, redlining, segregation, denying access, and discrimination. In her afterword in the book *Making Race Visible* (2003), Sonia Nieto argues, "Racism is a problem that must be confronted in research, in classroom practice, in the assumptions and beliefs that researchers and teachers have about the intelligence and capabilities of children of color." Based on work by Melissa Mosley and Rebecca Rogers (2011), we come to see how racism in classrooms is woven together throughout course materials; instructional activities, such as scripted activities requiring closed-ended responses; and classroom conversation traditions, such as metaphors, jokes, stories, and cultural narratives—for example, Black boys are better at sports than reading.

But most teachers are not intentionally engaging in racist acts toward individual students, so what is fueling this legacy of racism? Social psychologists would argue that it is the fallacy of our human cognition that allows racism to continue. More specifically, the cognitive strategy of categorizing information using mental shortcuts (called *heuristics*) is the culprit. In many aspects of our lives, these mental heuristics are helpful because they allow our minds to process a great deal of information quickly and to make decisions based on the data that is available (Tversky and Kahneman, 1974). We even use such mental heuristics to make social categorizations about people. But the problem is that these shortcuts can lead to faulty judgments, especially when our emotions are involved or when our minds have been programmed by society to misconstrue information. Because Americans' minds have been programmed by a society heavily steeped in racist beliefs, mental heuristics used for social categorizing of people and/or groups lead to stereotyping and racial prejudice. In fact, these societal stereotypes have contaminated our mental heuristics so much they have led to what social psychologists call *implicit racial bias*.

Most teachers are not intentionally engaging in racist acts toward individual students, so what is fueling this legacy of racism?

WHAT IS IMPLICIT RACIAL BIAS?

Implicit racial bias describes people's automatic, unconscious, negative responses toward people from racially marginalized social groups, such as Blacks, Jews, or Asians. Hundreds of studies confirm that implicit racial bias influences people's judgments, behavior, and decisions, such as voting (Greenwald et al., 2009; Payne et al., 2010), medical judgments (Green et al., 2007), and even whom to shoot in a video game (Correll, Park, Judd, and Wittenbrink, 2002).

Implicit racial bias: people's automatic, unconscious, negative responses toward people from racially marginalized social groups

But if these implicit racial biases are so strong, then how can we manage to live in a racially diverse society and interact with people from other social groups? Gaertner and Dovidio (1986) explain that racism has "gone underground" not only in society but also in people's minds. Over the past five decades, for example, American society has seen a decline in overt and deliberate expressions of racial bias (Dovidio, 2001; Schuman, Steeh, Bobo, and Krysan, 1997), which they call *explicit racial bias. Explicit racial bias* is the set of beliefs and values people are consciously aware that they possess and/or those beliefs and values they openly express. Unfortunately, however, since 2016 the United States has seen a sharp 17 percent increase in hate crimes, and these data are even more disheartening when we consider the fact that hate crimes are vastly underreported (Eligon, 2018). Yet, the magnitude and frequency of hate crimes perpetrated today are substantially less than the number of lynchings and cross-burnings that were prevalent in the early twentieth century.

Explicit racial bias: the set of beliefs and values people are consciously aware that they possess and/or those beliefs and values they openly express

During the civil rights movement of the 1940s to the 1970s, US federal legislative acts made it illegal to segregate Blacks or deny them education, housing, or voting rights. This movement also changed the social climate of the country in that people were less tolerant of openly expressed racist views or behavior, and such acts began to be viewed as immoral. (For discussion on this topic, see "Race in the American Mind: From the Moynihan Report to the Obama Candidacy" by Lawrence Bobo and Camille Charles in *The Annals of the American Academy of Political and Social Science,* volume 621, issue 1.) Just as social climate can curtail overt expressions of racism, it can also ignite such expressions if the cultural and political leadership allow bigotry to fester. Since 2016, the United States has not only seen the rise of hate crimes but also suffered a large White-nationalist rally in Charlottesville, Virginia, in 2017 that turned deadly.

Despite the recent heinous events, most Americans still admonish overt expressions of explicit racism. However, some Whites do report that "a lot of minorities are too sensitive," and those who express this belief are more likely to hold negative views of Blacks (Kanter et al., 2017). Several studies have asked people's opinions about race relations over the past decades. Bobo (2001) found that nearly all White Americans believe that Black and White children should be able to attend the same schools and that Blacks and Whites should be able to live in the same neighborhoods. Ironically, even though many people explicitly state nonbiased views related to schooling and housing, present-day schools and neighborhoods are still segregated to a significant degree. So, if people's openly stated racial attitudes are getting better, then why do the negative consequences of racism still exist?

Racism continues to exist because explicit racial bias and implicit racial bias are not always in sync. People might view themselves as unbiased but may be unaware of the unconscious biases they hold. In fact, it is quite common for people who claim to have unprejudiced views, nevertheless, to have implicit bias and act in racially biased ways during unclear or fearful situations (Banks and Hicks, 2016; Boysen and Vogel, 2008; Dovidio and Gaertner, 2000; Nosek et al., 2007). And unfortunately, implicit bias is a problem not only for White adults but also for children, even as young as age three. Research has shown that White youngsters show a preference for Whites over Blacks (Newheiser and Olson, 2012), demonstrate prejudiced attitudes and discriminatory behavior toward racial minorities (Aboud et al., 2012), and see Blacks as less human than Whites (Costello and Hodson, 2014). Even worse, people end up socializing with others who share similar attitudes, beliefs, and implicit racial biases (Sinclair, Kendrick, and Jacoby-Senghor, 2014; Towles-Schwen and Fazio, 2003).

HOW CAN TEACHERS CONTROL RACIAL BIAS?

The good news is that when people are motivated to control their biases, they can do so (Legault, Green-Demers, Grant, and Chung, 2007). Most people who are not prejudiced have a strong motivation to respond in unbiased ways. But having the emotional motivation is not enough. Because implicit racial bias is a deep-rooted problem in our thinking, people also need to develop mental strategies to stop biased thoughts, judgments, and decisions. Deprogramming training should intentionally try to foster positive emotions. People respond in less racially biased ways when they feel positive emotions as they interact with others, and these positive emotions are more likely to lead them to feel a sense of empathy for and connection to racial minorities (Dovidio and Gaertner, 2000; Dovidio et al., 2004).

Patricia Devine and colleagues (2002) explain that the first step in controlling our biases is to consciously decide that we do not want to act in biased ways and to then actively strive to adopt nonprejudiced beliefs and standards for personal behavior. Making a conscious decision to be unbiased goes a long way toward helping people control their explicit bias—what they say they believe or how they predict they might behave. The key to making this work is that the decision to act in a nonprejudiced manner must be based on one's own personal beliefs, not a decision made to please others or because one is succumbing to external pressures.

Controlling implicit bias, on the other hand, requires a person to engage in painstaking deprogramming steps. Such deprogramming consists of personalized education strategies, such as retraining your brain to no longer associate negative thoughts with a racial minority group. Typically, this deprogramming occurs through structured contact with members of a racial minority group. But these retraining strategies are time-consuming and emotionally taxing, especially for the racial minority members who are participating (Kawakami, Dovidio, and van Kamp, 2005; Sinclair, Kendrick, and Jacoby-Senghor, 2014; Shelton, West, and Trail, 2010). Such programs are important and key to changing people's ideas and opinions, but because they have the ability to make Whites as well as racial minorities feel emotionally vulnerable, they should only be offered by skilled professionals. It is important for such programs to be offered in a nonthreatening, low-stakes environment that allows teachers to practice new skills without feeling guilty, ashamed, or threatened with repercussions.

Other suggestions include expanding our shared realities by seeking opportunities for positive contact with other racial groups via diverse social networks. Humans need a sense of affiliation and certainty, and we achieve this through social interactions with people who provide us with consensus and affirmation. Unfortunately, as humans, we are notorious for seeking out people who are like us, and we will even adjust our own attitudes and beliefs to fit those of others within our social groups (Echterhoff, Higgins, and Levine, 2009). Being involved in racially and ethnically diverse social networks forces us to incorporate opposing points of view into our shared realities, and research has shown that exposing people to diverse group contact can also reduce implicit racial bias (Pettigrew, 2008; Tropp and Mallett, 2011). But this might actually be stressful, time-consuming, and emotionally depleting, especially for those who are members of a racial minority group (Richeson, Trawalter, and Shelton, 2005), given their smaller percentage of the American population and the widespread residential, workplace, and school segregation in the United States (Rugh and Massey, 2013). So racial minorities can end up feeling emotionally spent because they are often placed in work and social settings where they might be the only member of a minority group and therefore repeatedly face the burden of educating Whites. Instead, Sinclair, Kendrick, and Jacoby-Senghor (2014) suggest that nonbiased Whites intentionally show their non-biased beliefs and values when they are interacting with prejudiced peers and social contacts. Research shows Whites can play a key role in reducing bias if they stand up to other Whites and make their egalitarian views known (Sinclair, Kendrick, and Jacoby-Senghor, 2014). In situations such as this, Whites are showing themselves as allies in the fight for racial justice, and this can make a powerful statement and example to other Whites.

Let's do a check to see how ethnically and racially diverse your social network is.

Reflection Activity: Lemonheads and Whoppers—Is Your Everyday Life Racially and Ethnically Diverse?

The purpose of this activity is to begin thinking about your level of interaction with people of different races and ethnicities.

Materials Needed

1 piece of paper and a pen per person
A big box of Lemonhead candy to share
A big box of Whoppers candy to share
1 empty container for each person

What to Do

After each question asked by the facilitator, the participants will respond by placing either a Lemonhead or a Whopper candy into their containers. The Lemonheads will represent people of your own race or ethnicity. The Whoppers represent people from another racial or ethnic group.

> Who was the last guest invited to your house for dinner?

> Who was the last person you went out with socially?

> Who is your family doctor?

- Who is your family dentist?

- Who makes up the majority of students in the classes you take?

- Who makes up the majority of students in the classes you teach?
  (If you have not yet taught, the majority of students at the current/last university you attended.)

- Who is the professor who is your academic advisor or whom you spend the most time with?

- Who is your closest friend?

- Who is your current or previous romantic partner?

- Who is your spiritual leader?

- Who is/was your employer at your current/last job?

- Who makes up the majority of people at your favorite club/local hangout spot?

- Who made up the majority of people in your childhood community?

- Who is your favorite actor/actress?

- Who is your favorite singer/group?

Reflection Questions

On a piece of paper, respond to the following questions.

- What does your visual representation show you?

- Did you consider yourself to be someone who often interacted with others? Do you still?

- How diverse is your network? Is it more diverse in some aspects (such as work) but not others (such as your personal life)?

- If you have little to no exposure to people of a different racial or ethnic group, how can you make an effort to be more involved with others?

- Did you ever stop to think of how often you communicate with people outside your group?

- If you have little to no interaction with people outside your group, how does that affect your ability to teach in a diverse classroom?

CHALLENGING MISPERCEPTIONS

Adopting a culturally relevant anti-bias teaching pedagogy is fundamental when educating children of color. However, engaging in culturally relevant pedagogy (CRP) entails more than just adopting certain instructional practices and making sure your teaching materials are racially and ethnically diverse. To do CRP right, teachers have to do some soul searching and come to terms with the fact that implicit racial bias does in fact affect how they interact with children. So the first step on the way to using CRP is understanding the need to deprogram oneself to correct misperceptions of Black children and other children of color as learners.

Correcting teachers' misperceptions of children is critical because perceptions lay the foundation of teacher-student relationships, which we know are key to children's schooling success (Crosnoe et al., 2010). When teachers have positive perceptions of children, they are more likely to have positive interpersonal interactions with them (Davis, 2003), but when they have negative perceptions they are more likely to criticize children, call on them less often, or offer ineffective feedback (Brophy and Good, 1970; Good, 1981). Negative perceptions can also breed teacher-student conflict and poor student cooperation (Birch and Ladd, 1998), student underachievement (McCall, Evahn, and Kratzer, 1992), and poor child emotional adjustment (Ladd, Birch, and Buhs, 1999; Pianta, Steinberg, and Rollins, 1995).

Numerous studies reveal that teachers have different perceptions of children based on their race or ethnicity, and many of these perceptions are fraught with implicit racial bias. For instance, in studies by Clark McKown and Rhona Weinstein (2008), teachers' lower expectations for Black (and Latinx) children's academic performance in math and reading accounted for a wider year-end ethnic achievement gap. Even when Black (and non-White Latinx) children were high-achieving students, researcher Yasmiyn Irizarry (2015) found that teachers still had lower expectations for their academic literacy abilities in comparison to Whites. On the other hand, teachers perceive that Black children have more problem behaviors (Downey and Pribesh, 2004; Pigott and Cowen, 2000). Overall, Black children are viewed by adults as more culpable (Goff et al., 2014) and more aggressive (Todd, Thiem, and Neel, 2016) and are subject to harsher school discipline than their White counterparts (Okonofua and Eberhardt, 2015).

Not only are perceptions related to "ratings" of students, but also teachers' actual instructional behavior toward Black children is different (Murray, 1996). For instance, Black students receive fewer positive academic referrals, such as honors or gifted placement, but more negative referrals, such as special education or discipline-related sanctioning, in comparison to White and Asian students (Partenio and Taylor, 1985; Tenenbaum and Ruck, 2007). Teachers also direct more questions and encouragement to White students than they do to Blacks (Tenenbaum and Ruck, 2007).

Unfortunately, teachers' perceptions and behavior are much stronger predictors of Black students' perceptions of their own academic ability—an important predictor of academic success—than they are of White students' self-perceptions (Irvine, 1990). Aside from concerns about being stereotyped, minorities' intellectual engagement and performance are hindered by the mere concern that they do not belong (Walton and Cohen, 2007). Teachers' biased expectations for their minority students negatively impact student outcomes (Weinstein, Gregory, and Strambler, 2004).

Social identities are the categories that we place ourselves in that are shared with others, such as race, sex, religion, and sexual orientation (Tajfel and Turner, 1986). People experience social-identity threats when they are confronted with situations in which they perceive one or more of their social identities are attacked (Holmes, Whitman, Campbell, and Johnson, 2016). Substantial research on identity threats shows that the perception of bias can preoccupy minorities, siphoning away cognitive resources needed to optimally perform (Steele, Spencer, and Aronson, 2002). White instructors are more anxious and uncomfortable when interacting with Blacks, and this affects the quality of their teaching in an experimental situation (Jacoby-Senghor, Sinclair, and Shelton, 2016; Shelton, West, and Trail, 2010).

Social identities: the categories that we place ourselves in that are shared with others, such as race, sex, religion, and sexual orientation

The fact that teachers have these misperceptions is an ethical concern for the early education field because The National Association for the Education of Young Children (NAEYC) Code of Ethical Conduct (2011) says we are to do no harm. If we know that implicit bias is a problem throughout America, and we know that such bias negatively affects teachers' perceptions of children, stifles the teacher-child relationship, and leads to decreased learning outcomes for Black children, then we as leaders in our field and as individual teachers are knowingly inflicting harm on Black children because we are placing them in subpar learning environments.

Reflection Activity: Challenge Your Perceptions

The following lists contain various learning profiles that research has found to describe Black children's performance in school during the early grades. For these profiles, imagine Black children with whom you work who have diverse social-emotional needs and academic abilities. On a piece of paper, note how many children you think fit each profile. Describe your relationship with each child.

Boys

> A boy who is showing increasing academic ability in your class and who has average, age-appropriate social-emotional skills

> A gifted boy who entered your classroom with above-average academic and social-emotional skills and who is remaining consistently on this path

> A boy who is a lower achiever and is experiencing some social-emotional difficulties in the classroom

> A boy who entered your classroom as a high achiever but who is now showing declines socially and academically

Girls

> An average girl who has been staying on track with her academic and social-emotional growth

> A girl who is struggling both academically and social-emotionally

> A girl who is exceeding, above average both academically and socially-emotionally

DIVERSIFYING THE WORKFORCE
CAN HELP BLACK CHILDREN

Given that we know it is harmful for Black students to be educated by teachers who have negative perceptions and implicit bias, this fact is even more alarming considering the large teacher-student racial-ethnic mismatch that currently exists. Eighty percent of US teachers are White, even though more than 50 percent of children now served in public schools are non-White. Recruiting and retaining more Black teachers in the field could be beneficial to Black children in several ways.

First, research indicates that Black teachers have a more positive view of Black children than White teachers have. Black teachers, compared to Whites, rated Black students as less disruptive and having better work habits (Farkas, Grobe, Sheehan, and Shaun, 1990) and were less likely to recommend them for suspension (Dee, 2005). Black students perform consistently better when placed in Black teachers' classrooms (Egalite, Kisida, and Winters, 2015; Goldhaber and Hansen, 2010).

Also, Black teachers are more likely to understand through personal experience the trauma that racial bias can cause students (Kohli, 2009), and these teachers may be able to help children develop a positive racial identity. There is a positive link between positive racial identity and gifted achievement (Ford and Harris, 1997), reading and math scores on standardized tests (Smith, Atkins, and Connell, 2003), and positive school adjustment overall (Carter, 2008). This complexity and nuance of how Blacks communicate to children a positive sense of self-worth and racial pride, while at the same time communicating messages about racial inequalities and how to overcome such barriers, has been passed down in the culture from generation to generation (Bowman and Howard, 1985) and is a regular part of Black parenting (Crowley and Curenton, 2011; Curenton, Crowley, and Mouzon, 2018).

Having Black teachers would also be beneficial to Black children's education and development because they are more likely to form collaborative relationships with families and to establish and maintain culturally salient learning experiences (Iruka, Durden, and Kennel, 2015). Having Black teachers might lessen the incongruities that Black children feel between home and school. It is important to connect instruction to children's daily lives, such as including, valuing, and incorporating rituals and traditions; using similar mannerisms, interactions, or communication styles; and displaying respect toward adults in ways similar to their home and community environments. Also, instruction that is cooperatively focused, active, lively, with lots of opportunities for conversation and storytelling is beneficial for Black children (Gardner-Neblett, Pungello, and Iruka, 2012; Howard, 2001).

Reflection Activity: Getting Black Teachers into the Pipeline

> What does your program do to recruit, retain, and provide ongoing support to Black teachers?

> Name specific networking strategies.

> Name specific scholarships and/or funding sources for continued education and training.

> Name specific trainings your organization provides.

> How can you help to build the network of teachers of color in your program?

CHAPTER 4:

THE RESEARCH SUPPORT FOR CULTURALLY RESPONSIVE ANTI-BIAS EDUCATION

Recognizing White privilege, institutional racism, and bias is not enough. It is critical for education professionals to be able to implement culturally responsive anti-bias education to support all children's learning, especially Black children and other children of color.

More than thirty years ago, Louise Derman-Sparks and colleagues coined the term *anti-bias education* in their debut book, *Anti-Bias Education: Tools for Empowering Young Children*. Anti-bias education has become not only the buzzword in early childhood multicultural education but also the foundational framework for educational research and professional development within our field. The focus of the anti-bias framework was not only to address anti-bias practices and beliefs within and outside the early childhood classroom, but to provide children with tools, language, and skills to address biases that relate to gender, race, ethnicity, disability, and other characteristics. In essence anti-bias education began the conversation on the importance of, and how to go about creating, an anti-bias mindset in very young children. This work placed a spotlight on the role of early childhood professionals in explicitly addressing issues of racism, sexism, xenophobia, and homophobia with young children. This premise that young children bring with them and have the cognition and maturity to understand and be advocates for change in issues of bias and prejudice was novel, and it was viewed as developmentally inappropriate by many professionals in early childhood. In my own work within anti-bias research and professional development, educators have often commented that by introducing these topics to young children, we are introducing adult issues and doing more harm to their identity development and self-esteem—especially for children of color.

Research has documented that early childhood classrooms and programs can be places that represent institutional racism and inequitable learning practices through policies and practices that, for example, lead to disproportionately expelling Black children for the same behaviors as their White peers (US Department of Education, Office of Civil Rights, 2016). A 2017 study by Epstein, Blake, and Gonzalez concluded that Black girls routinely experience adultification bias as early as age five. *Adultification bias* is when adults believe Black girls need less protection, support, nurturing, and comfort than White girls (Epstein, Blake, and Gonzalez, 2017). Therefore, without a skilled teacher implementing practices that are affirming to young children, are anti-bias, and draw upon children's cultural tools, talents, and skills—practices promoted as developmentally appropriate—early childhood programs have the potential of doing more harm than good.

Undisputed, however, is the influence that the practices and rhetoric of anti-bias education have had on early childhood practices, policies, and research over the last three decades. Its popularity could greatly be attributed to being supported and published by the leading national early childhood professional organization, NAEYC. So, what is your position on anti-bias practices within early childhood education? Do you believe it is a developmentally and culturally appropriate framework to introduce to young children? How much do you understand about anti-bias education and how it intersects with culturally relevant teaching and best practices? As you reflect upon these questions, this chapter will focus on the what, so what, and now what of anti-bias education in the following ways:

> Examining why anti-bias education is important to integrate in classrooms today

> Introducing the primary components of anti-bias education and how it relates to educational theory and culturally relevant education

We will take a look at specific next steps that practitioners, educational and policy leaders, teacher educators, and researchers can take in advancing anti-bias efforts among children and adults.

Adultification bias: the view that Black girls need less protection, support, nurturing, and comfort than White girls

WHAT'S CULTURE GOT TO DO WITH IT?

Think about the last early childhood professional-development training you attended and/or led. What was the topic? Was it early literacy? effective family engagement? infant/toddler responsive care? How about addressing challenging behaviors with preschoolers? As these are leading topics in early childhood education, it wouldn't be a surprise if your last professional development focused on one of these areas. However, did any of these trainings discuss the role of children's culture and identity in their learning and development and overall long-term success? We in early childhood have subscribed to the golden principle that good teaching in the early years—implementing developmentally appropriate practices—will inevitably produce good results and child outcomes. Multicultural education emphasizes how such "good teaching" relies primarily on the cultures and home experiences of mostly middle-class White children. We'll look at some examples in a moment.

To ensure that all children have access to truly responsive teaching, intentional efforts must be made to identify how the curriculum, practices, and interactions are reflective of the cultures and home experiences of the children being served. The need is especially important in classrooms serving culturally and linguistically diverse (CALD) children; often, they see the culture, language, and experiences of their White peers but not their own. Research suggests that good teaching includes immersing students in their culture by using culturally affirming teaching practices that develop children who see themselves as cultural workers and leaders (Burchinal and Cryer, 2003; Carter, 2000; Durden, Escalante, and Blitch, 2015; Ladson-Billings, 1994, 2014). Such research shows that implementing culturally relevant and affirming educational experiences decreases the achievement and opportunity gaps between White and Black students. Startling, right? But when we critically explore our early childhood system and the practices we promote as "best" and "developmentally appropriate," they align almost exclusively within a Eurocentric cultural framework. Take for example an individualist versus collectivist perspective, as featured in Table 3.1, adapted from *Bridging Cultures in Early Care and Education: A Training Module*, by Zepeda, Rothstein-Fisch, Gonzalez-Mena, and Trumbull (2012).

Table 4.1. Individualist Perspective vs. Collectivist Perspective

Individualist	Collectivist
Stresses self-help: "You zipped up your jacket by yourself. Way to go!"	Sees the child as a member of a group; focuses on group esteem: "Look how awesome we are sitting crisscross applesauce."
Starts encouraging children to do things on their own at very early age; focuses on developing children's "inner controls" so they don't have to depend on adults for guidance.	Focuses on strengthening relationships and moving children away from independent urges; teaches that it is okay to depend on adults.
Recognizes achievement and expects a child to feel good about his or her accomplishments: "Look what a great job you did!"	Values modesty and humbleness; self-praise is considered bragging and is discouraged. Value is placed on group achievement.

What do you notice about the primary tenets of each perspective? Can you agree that the practices we promote in early childhood are primarily centered on individualist principles? This is problematic for two reasons. First, collectivist societies exist in Africa, Latin America, southern Europe, and East Asia. Collectivist cultures place a high value on group harmony, shared identities, and common goals and encourage behaviors that promote individuals getting along with others (Markus and Kitayama, 1998). In contrast, the individualist societies in western Europe, North America, and Australia emphasize individualism, autonomy, self-actualization, and personal uniqueness (Wang and Leichtman, 2000). As you may have noticed, America represents an individualist society; however, most culturally and linguistically diverse children are raised within collectivist-perspective families. Therefore, there is often a cultural clash that occurs but is not addressed between caregiving practices and educational goals and experiences between home and school.

The second issue is that our benchmarks of quality center on creating environments, teacher-child interactions, and child outcomes that encourage independence, self-help skills, and personal achievement. While these skills are important, this approach excludes the focus and goals of cooperative engagement and group goals and accomplishments that are valued by many cultural groups in our society.

Let's take a more practical look at how we subscribe to an individualist perspective in our work within early childhood. In most, if not all, early childhood programs, children will eat, play, and learn. Consider the following practices, discussed by Zepeda and colleagues, from an individualist perspective and from a collectivist perspective (Zepeda, et al., 2012).

> **Feeding and Dressing:**

  » **Individualist:** The developmental goal is independence. Adults encourage children to feed and dress themselves from infancy on and give children a certain amount of choice about what to eat and how much and about what to wear. Adults teach self-help skills and allow personal choice.

  » **Collectivist:** The developmental goal is *inter*dependence. Adults feed and dress babies and don't push them to feed and dress themselves, encouraging children to accept help. Obedience is emphasized over individual choice. Helping others is modeled. When self-help skills are encouraged, they derive from the desire to make the feeding or dressing process smoother for everybody involved, thereby promoting group harmony.

> **Learning and Play:**

  » **Individualist:** The developmental goal is independence; therefore, learning is child centered and involves play, exploration, and individual choice. Playing with objects and materials is a good way to learn about the physical world as well as about personal possessions. Children must first choose whether to understand themselves as possessors of objects before they can learn to share them. They are encouraged to share. Play is enjoyed between adults and children and among children.

  » **Collectivist:** The developmental goal is interdependence; therefore, learning is adult directed and depends more on observation than on play, exploration, and child choice. Objects are less important than relationships. Objects used in play are seen as a means of helping social interactions or teaching children to share. Sharing is stressed from the beginning of life; little emphasis is placed on personal ownership. Sharing is not a choice. Play most often occurs among siblings, cousins, or other children.

Now ask yourself the following questions in light of these examples:

> Which perspective do we encourage and promote as best practices in our field?

> How is this problematic to connecting to and building upon the cultural realities of all the children we serve?

> Think about the families you serve. Do you know whether children and families have collectivist or individualist practices and perspectives?

> Does representing both perspectives in the education of young children really matter in successful and long-term outcomes, especially for children from diverse backgrounds?

More than four decades of research suggests that, as learners, whenever we attempt to make sense of our world, we construct an understanding of an event by using our prior knowledge, past experiences, and cultural references or tools. Therefore, teaching and learning experiences must entail connecting to the cultural reality and experiences that children bring with them to the classroom. We must also examine how "doing business as usual" is affecting our ability to provide high-quality care and education for CALD children.

CHILDREN'S SOCIAL-CULTURAL AWARENESS

It's important to identify the development of children's social-cultural awareness and how starting early and young is critical to their long-term success. According to psychologist Lev Vygotsky's social-cultural theory, thinking and learning are highly influenced by language, social interactions, and culture (Driscoll and Nagel, 2008; Gonzalez-Mena, 2009). Vygotsky viewed development as social and collective rather than purely individual. *Social cognition*, or the cognitive process at play in our social interactions, involves a complex network of social, emotional, and cognitive development. Research shows the following:

> Infants are already aware of themselves, and toddlers at age two can express their feelings verbally (Umek, Kranjc, and Fekonja, 2000).

> Children go through a process of self-awareness, self-understanding, and understanding of others in which they notice gender, racial characteristics, and

physical disabilities during their third year of life (Derman-Sparks and ABC Taskforce, 1989; Derman-Sparks and Edwards, 2010). Young children become aware of what we consider racial characteristics, such as facial features, hair texture, eye shape, and skin color, and begin to acquire the language styles, customs, and behavioral codes of their ethnicity and culture long before they are able to label them as ethnic (Teaching Tolerance, 1997). As children develop their racial awareness, they acquire racial language to describe and categorize themselves and others. For example, my three-year-old recently said, "Mommy, you are yellow, Daddy is Black, and I am brown." When drawing a family picture, she uses a brown crayon to draw the three of us. To her, she has identified the shades of brown our family represents while also drawing upon the racial vocabulary she has heard from adults and possibly her peers. Conceptual inconsistencies between these two sets of terms, black and brown, is reflected in the way she labels what she notices and in the application (using a brown crayon) of these terms.

> Children two-and-a-half to three years old become aware of and begin to take in socially prevailing negative ideas, feelings, and stereotypes about people and about themselves (Derman-Sparks, 1993; Derman-Sparks and Edwards, 2010).

Current anti-bias literature tells us that racial prejudice in young children leads to distortion of judgment and perception of reality and can be both external and internal. In other words, children can learn discriminatory practices from external negative sources, such as from adults or peers, but children also consistently and naturally act in discriminatory ways and display prejudicial attitudes. To illustrate, as children perceive the world through an egocentric lens, they may respond to children who are different from them using prejudice or negative words, such as *dirty*, *mean*, *bad*, or *ugly*. "Don't play with stinky Kendall." "White people are mean." "Diana talks funny."

On the other hand, a child's interactions with parents, other children, community, and caregivers will inevitably shape his perception and judgment of others different from himself. If these interactions are negative, the child can develop prejudicial beliefs and practices. The following reflective questions help to illuminate this point.

Consider the last children's book you read to young children.

> What were the physical characteristics of the main character (weight, age, ability, skin tone, hair texture, eye shape, primary language)?

> How does this one book communicate a positive self-image of a child or children in your classroom or program?

Key point: Sometimes, when we do not include positive images that look like the children we teach, we communicate that who they are and the talents they bring to the classroom are not important.

Consider a conversation between a parent and child while shopping:

Milian, four years old, points at the Chinese clerk while his mother is checking out an item and asks, "Mom, why does her eyes look funny?"

The mother responds, "Oh, don't say that. It's not nice." She mumbles, "I'm sorry," to the cashier and pulls a wide-eyed Milian out of the store.

Key point: Not addressing the child's natural curiosity or inquiry communicates that the difference is wrong and should not be accepted. Instead the parent could have responded, "Why do you say her eyes look funny?" Upon the child's reply, which will likely be about the shape of the cashier's eyes, the parent can instead point to her own eyes or find a nearby reflection and say, "Look at our eyes. You get your eye shape from mommy and daddy. See? Maybe she get's her eye shape from her mommy and daddy, too. It's awesome that we have different eye shapes that we get from our family. Our eyes may be different, but they help us to see." The parent can then briefly bring in the cashier on the conversation by asking her the question directly: "Did you get your eye shape from your mommy and daddy?" This quick three-minute teachable moment explicitly addresses the curiosity the child has about difference while also communicating a positive perspective rather than communicating bias or encouraging a prejudicial belief.

EMPATHY, CULTURAL AWARENESS, AND INTERNALIZED PREJUDICE

Throughout childhood, children continue to develop and elaborate on their ideas on the identity of others, feelings about human differences, and their feelings about their own cultural identity. *Empathy*—being aware of and sensitive to the feelings and experiences of others—is closely related to the theory of the mind and the development of social cognition.

As Umek and researchers (2000) assert, the development and encouragement of empathy allows children to reflect on these feelings and ideas. Children as young as three years old are able to empathize with others if they have experienced, indirectly or directly, similar feelings or emotional responses from the people around them (Umek, Kranjc, and Fekonja, 2000).

Theory of the mind: the understanding that others have feelings, thoughts, perspectives, beliefs, and opinions that differ from one's own

For example, consider the following scenarios. Maria, four years old, sees a stereotypical "Indian warrior" figure in a toy store. "That toy hurts Indian people's feelings," she tells her grandmother. Maria empathizes with the feelings of Native American people. However, of greater importance is that Maria is able to determine that the toy would hurt the Native American's feelings, for this understanding had to occur prior to her empathizing with their feelings. Either Maria is herself a Native American or she has been exposed to teaching that supports sensitivity to other cultures.

Paul, a four-year-old, and his mother are at the grocery store one evening, and Paul is pretending to be his favorite action hero, Spider-Man. He pretends to zap the canned foods and says, "Got ya! Got ya! I save the day again!" Paul then notices a young Black man walking down the grocery aisle and proceeds to zap the man playfully. His mother is startled but also amused; she comments, "Paul, it's not nice to zap people." Paul responds, "I must save the world from this very bad man! Rah rah rah!" Shocked, Paul's mother shushes Paul and moves him down the aisle.

What does this vignette demonstrate? Could you clearly see a young boy playing in the aisle, imitating his favorite action hero? Do the following *what ifs* come to mind?

> What if Paul is directly connecting this person's race to being bad rather than good?

> What if Paul has internalized the stereotype often portrayed in society, books, and the media that Black men are dangerous criminals and bad?

> What if his mother had taken a moment and asked, "Well, why do you think this man is bad?"

> Would our perception of the intent of this comment differ based on the child's race?

Research tells us that in occurrences where prejudice and stereotypes have distorted a child's perception of others, young children have the intellectual capacity for undoing any pre-existing unfair perceptions of others as they engage in meaningful experiences (Hyun, 2003b). That's good news! Child-care providers and parents can use teachable moments and developmentally and culturally appropriate practices to address the prejudice, stereotypes, and negative perceptions young children may have developed. The mission and vision of educators should thus be to provide teachable moments that develop into authentic learning moments. Teachers need training to equip them with immediate and appropriate reactions to children who display prejudicial, stereotypical, or racist actions toward themselves or others. As addressed, research supports the claim that all children, regardless of ethnicity, ability, or economic status, are able to empathize and be sensitive to others different from themselves if schooled and nurtured in an environment that celebrates, acknowledges, and respects diversity.

Acknowledging this cognitive and affective ability is important as it suggest how children are capable of understanding and learning anti-bias principles. Anti-bias education is for the benefit of all children and has the potential to make this world a more socially just, equitable, and affirming place for all to live. Educators must address children's negative perceptions when they arise and also create intentional opportunities to teach anti-bias principles and engage children in culturally relevant educational experiences. In our next chapter, we will look at how to do this.

> All children, regardless of ethnicity, ability, or economic status, are able to empathize and be sensitive to others different from themselves if schooled and nurtured in an environment that celebrates, acknowledges, and respects diversity.

CHAPTER 5:

LIGHTS, CAMERA, TEACH! KEY FEATURES OF ANTI-BIAS EDUCATION

CULTURALLY RELEVANT EDUCATION

How do we as educators intentionally engage children in culturally relevant educational experiences? Social cultural theory requires teachers to view all learning experiences through the cultural lens of the child because learning is culturally mediated. *Looking through the lens of the child* means that teachers implement curriculum and instructional practices that are culturally sensitive and relative to the child's experience. As described by Gay (2000, 2002) and Howard (2003), *culturally relevant pedagogy* (CRP) entails connecting learning and classroom experiences to children's home conversations and experiences. To effectively implement a culturally relevant and sustainable pedagogy, teachers and early care programs must establish the following attitudes:

> Believe that all students can succeed.

> Focus on maintaining affirming student-teacher relationships.

> See excellence as a complex standard that accounts for student diversity and individual difference (Paris, 2012).

Culturally relevant pedagogy connects classroom learning to children's home experiences and native languages (Ladson-Billings 2014). Cultural understanding of students—family traditions, customs, and so on—is important, but alone it is not sufficient. Culturally relevant teachers help students make connections between students' community, national, and global identities and how these identities are impacted by racism, sexism, and oppression (Paris, 2012). They also encourage children to work collaboratively and expect them to teach and take responsibility for each other (Ladson-Billings, 1995, 2014). The following is an overall summary of the primary components of culturally relevant teaching and education.

> ## Conceptions of Self and Others

>> The teacher sees herself as an artist and teaching as an art.

>> The teacher sees herself as part of the community and teaching as giving something back to the community. The teacher encourages children to do the same.

>> The teacher believes all children can learn.

>> The teacher helps children make connections between their community, national identities, and global identities.

>> The teacher sees teaching as "pulling knowledge out," like mining.

> ## Social Relations

>> The teacher-student relationship is fluid and humanely equitable and extends to interactions beyond the classroom and into the community.

>> The teacher demonstrates a connectedness with all students.

>> The teacher encourages a community of learners.

>> The teacher encourages children to learn collaboratively. Students are expected to teach each other and be responsible for each other.

> ## Conceptions of Knowledge

>> Knowledge is continuously re-created, recycled, and shared by teachers and students. It is not static or unchanging.

>> Knowledge is viewed critically.

>> The teacher is passionate about content.

>> The teacher helps children develop necessary skills.

>> The teacher seeks excellence as a complex standard that takes student diversity and individual differences into account.

(Ladson-Billings, 1994)

So what do these components actually look like within real classrooms with real teachers and children? Check out below what I will call Ms. Brown's and Ms. Taylor's preschool classroom. Can you identify the elements of culturally relevant teaching?

CULTURALLY RELEVANT EDUCATION
IN ACTION

When you enter Ms. Brown's and Ms. Taylor's classroom, the first thing you notice are pictures of the children and their families (created by the families) displayed on the cabinets at the children's eye level. As a vistor you would immediately look at each child's family collage and see the unique interests and familial connections of each child. If you take a look around the classroom's environment, you will notice that the dolls, figurines, and toys represent multiple shades of brown, pink, and yellow and have various hair textures. The classroom is physically set up with sturdy and wide chairs, cushions, and pillows to allow an adult to comfortably sit at eye level with a child. Tables and play areas are arranged to encourage collaborative and cooperative group work and experiences. Some brightly colored children's books invite children to explore the world of dinosaurs. Other beautifully illustrated books promote self-love. *Dream Big, Little One* acknowledges the contributions of African American women in society. You may hear soft jazz playing during nap time or oral storytelling by teachers, children, and guests during story time.

You will hear multiple languages spoken in the classroom and see written words in these languages as well. The teachers are excited to introduce other languages, such as French, Mandarin Chinese, Spanish, and Arabic, in their majority native-English-speaking classroom; therefore, you will hear fingerplays and songs like the one below from Ghana. You will see labels on the shelves, bookcases, and displays in these languages, too. You will hear the children and teachers speaking variations of the English language as children bring with them dialects and vocabulary that both extend and complement the standard English language. For example, you may hear, "Give me dat dere," or "Can I have the book por favor, chica?" "Hola, Jessica! What are your favorite meals you like to eat? Who cooks them? Do you help sometimes?" You will also see children and teachers using their hands, facial expressions, an eyebrow raised, verbal clicks and ticks, and "Umm-humms" to express and communicate their thoughts, needs, dislikes, agreements, and approvals. These multiple literacies are both encouraged and celebrated.

> **Leader:** *Kye Kye Kule* (Pronounced *chay chay koo-lay*; put hands on head)
> **Chorus:** *Kye Kye Kule* (put hands on head)
>
> **Leader:** *Kye Kye Kofinsa* (*chay chay koh-feen sah*; put hands on shoulders)
> **Chorus:** *Kye Kye Kofinsa* (put hands on shoulders)
>
> **Leader:** *Kofisa Langaa* (*Koh-fee sah lahn-gah*; put hands on waist)
> **Chorus:** *Kofisa Langaa* (put hands on waist)
>
> **Leader:** *Kaka Shilanga* (*Kah-kah shee lahn-gah*; put hands on knees)
> **Chorus:** *Kaka Shilanga* (put hands on knees)

Leader: *Kum Aden Nde* (*koom ah-dehn day*; put hands on ankles)
Chorus: *Kum Aden Nde* (put hands on ankles)

Leader: *Kum Aden Nde* (put hands on ankles)
Chorus: *Kum Aden Nde, HEY!* (put hands on ankles, shout *hey* and stand up)

English translation:

Hands on your head
Hands on your shoulders
Hands on your waist
Hands on your knees
Hands on your ankles
Hands on your ankles, hey!

Ms. Brown and Ms. Taylor value the strengths of the children, families, and community. They demonstrate this by intentionally seeking opportunities to learn from the children, families, and the community and by participating in local events when possible. Families make a point of inviting the teachers: "Hi there, Ms. Jones. I hear there is a community block party going on this weekend. Do you know about it?" The teachers' interactions with the family go beyond pickup and drop-off and represent a village or communal engagement. Teachers and parents respect one another and the role each plays in caring for and educating the children. Therefore, each adult works hard to effectively communicate with the other adults about each child's progress, strengths, and areas of improvement. The teachers offer flexible meeting times to accommodate busy family schedules: "Can't come to parent-teacher conference due to your work schedule? Let's meet Saturday morning at Waffle House, or I'll give you a call after church on Sunday."

Instead of creating and outlining teaching experiences and activities that teach toward objectives and standards, all planning, implementation, and assessment starts and ends with what the children know and what they are interested in learning and exploring. Ms. Brown and Ms. Taylor firmly believe that to teach is to learn more from the children and the families and use this knowledge to build upon what children know to extend their learning. The objectives and standards are guides, only peripherally used for a baseline, as children are capable of—and are expected to achieve—far more in their learning and application.

When you have the opportunity to observe the teaching and learning in Ms. Brown's and Ms. Taylor's classroom, you see children who have multiple peer playmates. You see teachers who easily flow among children engaging in authentic and responsive conversations. It is not uncommon for the children to take on the role of the teacher or knowledge giver. Children are encouraged to ask why, and teachers routinely ask children why and encourage them to explain their thoughts, ideas, and hypotheses about the world and individuals around them. Ms. Brown and Ms. Taylor believe that each child brings a unique set of cultural skills, strength, and knowledge to the classroom, and they become excited by the challenge each year to explore with children ways to build upon and extend these skills and knowledge. Here, a child who might be labled in other classrooms as bossy and disrespectful in her challenging or talking back to teachers is viewed instead as having distinguished skills in critical thinking, leadership, and the intrinsic courage for advocacy. A child who might be labled in another classroom as hyperactive, unable to sit still and focus, is viewed as one whose energy can be channeled toward creative expression in movement and hands-on explorations. She can be encouraged to create, build, or develop innovative, out-of-the box strategies and solutions—a future innovator, designer, or entrepreneur.

In all, the activities and interactions in this classroom are rooted in the lived experiences and interests of the children. For example, when reading a book about gardening, the children overwhelmingly expressed interest in creating a garden, as none of them had one at their home or had seen one in their community. To make this topic relevant to the children, Ms. Brown and Ms. Taylor decided to first explore which fruits and vegetables each child eats at home and how their families get these food items. The teachers would use this information to help children see beyond the classroom to exploring the benefits of having a home or community garden, including exploring with the children why home or community gardens don't exist in some areas and what they could do to create one.

Reflection Questions

In this brief example, are you able to identify components of culturally relevant teaching? What are the specific tangible practices, and what are the "hidden" or implicit beliefs and values of Ms. Brown and Ms. Taylor that undergird their practice? As you consider this scenario, think about your own interactions with young children or the adults who serve young children. How can you create more culturally responsive spaces and experiences for young children? What are the beliefs and practices you must change in order for this to occur?

Intentionally, the last example provided in this scenario about home and community gardens segues nicely into the next topic about anti-bias education. If you have knowledge about anti-bias education, why do you think this particular example demonstrates an anti-bias educational experience for children?

ANTI-BIAS EDUCATION

Culturally relevant education made its debut in the early 1990s and focused primarily on implementing experiences for elementary-age children backed by research conducted on highly successful teachers of Black children. In the late 1980s, Louise Derman-Sparks and the ABC Task Force (1989) proclaimed that within early childhood—particularly during the early years—we should infuse children's culture in the classroom while simultaneously developing their awareness of how color, gender, language, and physical ability are greatly connected to power and privilege. This practice is known as *anti-bias education*, and Derman-Sparks, in her article "Empowering Children to Create a Caring Culture in a World of Differences" (1993), argues that children should have experiences that develop anti-bias attitudes, engage them in critical pedagogy, and teach them how to speak out against injustice. Therefore, to take on such an active approach in challenging stereotypes, bias, and prejudice, scholars suggest teachers must not only implement culturally relevant practices but also must infuse these across disciplines. Cultural explorations should not be exclusive to celebrating holidays or what Derman-Sparks (1993) refers to as *tourist curriculum practices.* A *tourist curriculum* is defined as one that patronizes and trivializes a group of people.

The real-life experiences and everyday realities of people from different cultures are not captured in this approach. In their book *Anti-Bias Education for Young Children and Ourselves,* Louise Derman-Sparks and Julie Olsen Edwards argue, instead, that teachers should celebrate the comprehensive diversity of students—their family styles, genders, physical differences, cultures, and so on—by employing culturally affirming and relevant practices. The environment should include pictures and posters of children, parents, and staff who are in the program. Displays should also represent other racial and ethnic groups. Pictures and posters should include students with disabilities, elderly people, and men and women in various recreational and working capacities, such as men as nurses, women as firefighters, and so on. Toys and materials should reflect diversity in gender roles, racial and cultural backgrounds, special needs, occupations, and age ranges. Diversity can be most powerfully reflected in books and music selections, with dolls, and with art materials. The environment should also be equipped with mirrors so that children have opportunities to check out their physical appearances. Not only are these practices "good teaching," but they also help to encourage young children's sociocultural awareness, positive racial and cultural identities, and empathy of others.

To help further stimulate children's sensitivity toward others different from themselves and to promote sociocultural and equitable learning experiences, Curenton and Iruka (2013) developed the culturally relevant anti-bias framework, which emphasizes the need for teachers to actively engage in issues focused on social justice, democracy, and human rights; strive for an equitable distribution of participation and power between teacher and children; and acknowledge, reject, and challenge racism, classim, sexism, and other forms of oppression. Caregivers should offer immediate and appropriate response to students who display biased behavior. Take, for example, the following scenarios. How would you respond?

After hearing a children's book during story time about a heroic princess with long blonde hair, Kim, age three, goes to the dramatic play area and puts a baby blanket on her head. She exclaims, "I'm beautiful now!"

Ms. Walker responds, "Well, I think your hair is beautiful, curly, and brown. I love it!"

Kim shouts, "No! It's not! I have pretty, long hair now!"

––––––––––––

After being taken to see a popular children's film, five-year-old Marcus exclaims, "I'm glad I'm not as dark as Shari (his older sister)." Then he adds sadly, "Dark people are bad and mean." His uncle is puzzled because all the cartoon characters were animals, but then he realizes that the bad, evil, or mischievous animals were dark, and all the good and heroic animals were golden or bronze.

Reflection Questions

> How would you respond to Kim?

> How would you respond to Marcus?

In situations where you are unsure of how to respond, it is okay to take a step back and reflect on possible responses. If needed, talk over some possible responses with a trusted friend or colleague. However, **always** go back to the child with your new response.

In an anti-bias classroom, all children are supported in their preferred learning styles and encouraged to try new ways of interacting with people and materials (Sparks, 1993). The next section outlines the educational goals and principles of anti-bias education and provides specific and practical examples of how this applies to teaching and learning.

ANTI-BIAS EDUCATIONAL GOALS

Derman-Sparks and Edwards (2010) list four goals of anti-bias education.

Goals: Each child will demonstrate self-awareness, confidence, family pride, and positive social identity. Each child will express comfort and joy with human diversity; accurate language for human differences; and deep, caring human connections.

Practice: Encourage children to notice and appreciate their own physical traits and those of others:

> Provide hand-held mirrors to let children inspect their own faces and a large mirror at child level so they can see full-size images of themselves and others.

> Affirm children's curiosity about their own and others' races or ethnicities. For example, if three-year-old Maria, a Latina child, asks, "I'm a *chica*, yes?" Say, "Yes," and point out unique and relevant facts such as the number of langues she speaks, her beautiful skin color, and her family's unique cultural traditions.

Goal: Each child will increasingly recognize unfairness, have language to describe unfairness, and understand that unfairness hurts.

Practice: Intentionally create learning experiences that assess children's sterotypes and misconceptions. For example, what are their thoughts and feelings about a person who is deaf, homeless, or of a different race? Take note of the comments children make during play, informal conversations, or conversations after hearing books that explicitly feature characters with these characteristics.

Plan activities that not only bring out negative beliefs and thoughts about others but also help develop children's emphathy and fairness. Encourage the development of critical-thinking skills that pave the way for them to learn how to take action. For example, ask the children to identify something meaningful that they could do in the school or community, such as picking up litter, inspecting the building for accessiblity to the physically challenged, or creating an accessible community garden. Talk with them about how the action promotes fairness. Then, do it! (Teaching Tolerance, 1997)

Goal: Each child will demonstrate empowerment and the skills to act, with others or alone, against prejudice and/or discriminatory actions.

Practice: This goal requires teachers to directly intervene to support a child who has been hurt by biased behavior and to also help children learn alternative ways of interacting. First, be alert to any unfair practices that directly impact children's lives, whether they are done by the school—prohibiting or correcting children for using native or home language in the classroom, for example—or by peers—such as name calling.

Create spaces that are conducive to talking and listening about issues of prejudice and discrimation. These spaces could take the form of a circle for groups or private areas for one-on-one discussions. Encourage whole-group dialogue among children rather than teacher-child question and response.

Design learning activities that help children explore the concepts of justice and fairness by using dramatic play, puppets, or props to talk about fairness and justice. Read selected children's books, such as *Amazing Grace* by Mary Hoffman, to discuss and act out hypothetical social and moral problems or issues of prejudice and discrimination.

EDUCATIONAL PRINCIPLES FOR PUTTING ANTI-BIAS GOALS INTO ACTION

Derman-Sparks and Edwards (2010) offer some foundational educational principles that will help you put the four anti-bias goals into action.

> The four anti-bias education goals are for everyone, and everyone benefits.

  Translation: Bias and societal inequities impact all children; some benefit and others are oppressed by them. Anti-bias education provides the tools and consciousness to disrupt these inequitities and provides positive identity supports for children of color.

> Anti-bias education activities pay attention to the realities of children's lives.

  Translation: Anti-bias educators design experiences based on the cultural backgrounds of the children and families they serve.

> Anti-bias education is developmentally appropriate.

  Translation: Anti-bias educators choose learning experiences that are cognitively, socially, and emotionally accessible to young children. These experiences allow them to explore new ideas and understandings of complex topics.

> Anti-bias planning uses both child- and teacher-initiated activities.

Translation: Anti-bias educators must be both *reactive*, responding to child-initiated activities, and *proactive*, providing intentionally created activities.

> Anti-bias learning does not happen in one lesson or one day.

Translation: Anti-bias education is the basis and foundation for everything that happens in your classroom. Children must have many opportunities to engage in anti-bias learning and experiences.

> Anti-bias education calls on teachers to know themselves.

Translation: Teachers must broaden their understanding of themselves and others. They must recognize and acknowledge their own biases and prejudices to be able to identify them when they occur in the classroom—whether done by themselves or the children.

> Anti-bias education avoids the pitfalls of a tourist curriculum.

Translation: Anti-bias education is not an occasional or seasonal superficial experience. For example, only talking about discrimination during Black History Month or discussing civil rights as an issue of the past is not sufficient.

> Anti-bias education rests on strong relationships among staff and between staff and families.

Translation: Anti-bias education is key to raising the same issues of fairness and equity with other caregivers who engage with children in your program.

CONNECTING THE DOTS:
CULTURALLY RELEVANT EDUCATION
+ ANTI-BIAS EDUCATION

Anti-bias education and culturally relevant education both came on the educational scene almost thirty years ago. The target audience for anti-bias education was early childhood professionals (primarily preschool professionals), and the audience for culturally relevant teaching was elementary teachers. There have been various applications of each of these frameworks that have extended beyond the targeted audience and educational fields, a change that speaks to the importance and significance of this work. When thinking about how these two frameworks connect, consider the metaphor of baking a pound cake.

For the pound cake to come out golden and delicious, not only do you have to include the right amount of ingredients, soul, and love during the mixing process, but you must also set the oven to the right temperature and provide ongoing monitoring to make sure the cake is rising to expectations (and beyond). Consider culturally relevant pedagogy (CRP) as the mixing process and anti-bias education as the baking process. CRP provides a clear guideline on the beliefs needed to subscribe to an education that values and honors the cultural genius and educational excellence of CALD children. There are also examples in research on how teachers can make learning more meaningfully and culturally relevant for children. However, without the right ingredients of teacher-affirming beliefs, competencies, and skills in implementing CRP—and a commitment to speaking out against culturally subtractive policies, such as curriculum and assessment imposed upon young children—the cake is doomed to failure and will not rise. When a teacher is equipped with a theory of mind focused on culturally relevant education and on explicitly addressing issues of biases, stereotypes, and prejudices with young children (that is, the right temperature, and the right amount of love, care, and intentionality), then the teacher can maximize children's educational success and ability to evoke change.

So, what next? We have at our disposal decades of research and strategies for implementing CRP and anti-bias education, but where do we begin?

NOW WHAT?

TOOLS TO MOVE FORWARD

KNOW YOURSELF

Hyun (2003a) notes that for teachers to begin and then maintain a culturally relevant and anti-bias program, they must develop a conscious awareness of their own multiple identities:

> ➤ Ethnically: as a member of a race or races, and/or as a member of a particular social or national group or groups

> Linguistically: as a person who speaks a language or languages

> Culturally: as a member of a group that has distinct cuisine, language, arts, religious beliefs, social norms, and/or achievements

> Gender: as a person on the gender spectrum

> Socioeconomically: as a person who has been affected by a combination of social and economic factors

Teachers must also be willing to step back and critically re-examine their own interpretations and beliefs of the identities of the children they teach (Banks, 2004; Cochran-Smith, 2004). Teachers can begin this examiniation by completing the privilege-walk activity discussed in chapter 2 on pages 39–40 and by engaging in the "Where I'm From" poem activity. They can also participate in implicit-bias trainings or workshops. This activity is based on the poem "Where I'm From" by George Ella Lyon, a writer, teacher, and former poet laureate for the Commonwealth of Kentucky. You can find the poem on her website http://georgeellalyon.com/where. html, where she recommends using the poem as a starting point for looking at your own origins and engaging in self-reflection. Learn more about the I Am From Project, developed by Lyon and author and retired teacher Julie Landsman, at https://iamfromproject.com.

"I Am From" Activity

1. Read the poem, "Where I'm From" by George Ella Lyon, available at http://georgeellalyon.com/where.html

2. Notice that she includes specific details representing her culture and ethnicity: food, family names, and location.

3. Next, write your own poem. Include three characteristics that represent your culture and ethnicity.

Poem by T. R. Durden

I'm from a place of pine trees,
scraped knees and disguised poverty.
I am the rhythm of the Nile,
soul of the drum and brilliance of Bertha's smile.
I am the peach
that drips with sweet memories
from the spirits overseas.

I'm from hot, humid summers
Sit down, be still in lightning and thunder
I'm from switch the code to code the switch
From dis iz it to this is it

I'm from the place they call the Dirty South
not ashamed by the southern swag spilling from my mouth.
I'm from the place of broken dreams
whips and chains
The place of we shall overcome
and Rise Again.

Too young for the Jim Crow threats
Just right for Black Lives Matter—oh yes!

Use this activity to discover your primary identities that shape the lens through which you view children and families who are similar to or different from yourself.

CONSIDER YOUR PROGRAM

Professionals have few opportunities to experience professional development and training that explicitly explores how a child's culture and language can and should be the basis for all teaching, learning, and assessment. For example, how often do teachers and leaders question the current early childhood measures of quality to identify how they do or do not represent an individualist versus collectivist view of teaching, learning, and parenting?

Take a look at your own classroom or program. Are there structural issues within curriculum, policies, and assessment that benefit some children in your program more than others? Critically reflect on your own practice and work with children. Is it equitable? Does it reflect and build upon children's unique cultures, languages, and communal experiences? Does your teaching reflect a one-size-fits-all approach disguised as best practices or developmentally appropriate practice?

If you are a practitioner, teacher educator, researcher, or educational leader, explore the following resources to add to your teaching toolbox as a guide for implementing CRP and anti-bias practices.

It is critical for teachers to reflect on how their current instructional program and the educational environment may or may not contribute to student discrimination and cultural disconnect.

Curenton, Stephanie, and Iheoma U. Iruka. 2013. *Cultural Competence in Early Childhood Education*. San Diego, CA: Bridgepoint Education.

Derman-Sparks, Louise. 1989. *Anti-Bias Curriculum: Tools for Empowering Young Children*. Washington, DC: NAEYC.

Derman-Sparks, Louise, and Julie O. Edwards. 2010. *Anti-Bias Education for Young Children and Ourselves*. Washington, DC: NAEYC.

Durden, Tonia, Elsa Escalante, and Kimberly Blitch. 2014a. *Culture Matters: Strategies to Support Young Children's Social and Cultural Development.* (Guide for teachers.) Lincoln, NE: University of Nebraska–Lincoln Extension, Institute of Agriculture and Natural Resources. Available at http://extensionpublications.unl.edu/assets/pdf/g2241.pdf

Durden, Tonia, Elsa Escalante, and Kimberly Blitch. 2014b. *Culture Matters: Strategies to Support Your Young Child's Social and Cultural Development.* (Guide for parents.) Lincoln, NE: University of Nebraska–Lincoln Extension, Institute of Agriculture and Natural Resources. Available at http://extensionpublications.unl.edu/assets/pdf/g2242.pdf

Iruka, Iheoma, Stephanie Curenton, and Tonia Durden, eds. 2017. *African American Children in Early Childhood Education: Making the Case for Policy Investments in Families, Schools, and Communities.* Bingley, UK: Emerald Publishing.

Teaching Tolerance Project and Southern Poverty Law Center. 1997. *Starting Small: Teaching Tolerance in Preschool and the Early Grades.* (Film and teacher guide.) Montgomery, AL: Southern Poverty Law Center. https://www.tolerance.org/classroom-resources/film-kits/starting-small

Slavin, Robert, Nancy Madden, and Barbara Wasik. 1996. "Roots and Wings: Universal Excellence in Elementary Education." In *Bold Plans for School Restructuring: The New American Schools Designs.* Mahwah, NJ: Lawrence Erlbaum and Assoc.

KNOW THE CHILDREN IN YOUR CLASSROOM

It is critical for teachers to both acknowledge and examine how and whether the stereotypes, prejudices, and beliefs we often see perpetuated within larger society are mirrored in their classrooms. As negative biases and inequity seep into the fabric of our educational system, opportunities for quality and equitable educational experiences for CALD children diminish (Hilliard, 2000).

What are the educational inequities that have impacted the success and educational experiences of CALD children? Often young CALD children are not assessed or taught in their native languages, despite literature and research to suggest that building upon children's multiple literacies and languages not only enhances cognitive development and learning but also contributes to long-term gains and positive outcomes (Boutte, 2012, 2015; Smitherman, 2000; Smitherman and Villanueva, 2003). A disproportionate number of African American preschool boys are expelled from preschool and/or tracked into special education. Current research suggests this is the result of stereotypes and biases projected upon these children by their teachers (Hathaway, 2016).

In addition to examining your own ways of knowing and cultural being through activities such as the "Where I'm From" activity, it is also important to explicitly explore how you may be unconsciously engaging in implicit-bias interactions with young children. There is a great free resource developed by the University of Nebraska Extension called *Say What? Understanding, Identifying, and Addressing Microaggressions* (Kok et al., 2015). This tool will help you focus on identifying microaggressions and biased beliefs that you may unknowingly project onto others. It also offers strategies for addressing microaggressions if you experience them or witness them occurring. You can find the resource here:

> Participant guide: http://extensionpublications.unl.edu/assets/pdf/hef616.pdf

> Facilitator/leader guide: http://extensionpublications.unl.edu/assets/pdf/hef617.pdf

CONCLUDING THOUGHTS AND A CALL TO ACTION

In addition to critically reflecting on our own biases and stereotypical beliefs, teachers must come to understand, appreciate, and show sensitivity to cultural differences as they interact with students and parents in the classroom. Various tools can assist in this process. For example, as mentioned earlier, Curenton and Iruka (2013) developed the culturally relevant anti-bias framework, which promotes teaching as incorporating the cultural experiences, knowledge, and communication styles of diverse learners. Researchers and early childhood leaders must examine the current measures we use to assess high-quality classroom environments and teacher-child interactions. Tools are currently being developed that help to measure culturally relevant education in preschool classrooms, such as the *Assessing Classroom Sociocultural Equity Scale* by Stephanie Curenton, Bryant Jensen, Iheoma Iruka, Tonia Durden, and Marisha Humphries. A plethora of research is being done on innovative practices and interventions that draw upon culturally relevant and anti-bias principles.

Our educational policy should include recruiting and retaining culturally educated and competent teachers and training and providing ongoing professional development—no exceptions. If we have the will to educate all children, then we must be intentional in our work of recruiting and supporting the best and most promising teachers who express an interest and have skill in teaching CALD children. We must be effective, motivated, resilient, and transformative. We need teachers who engage in and seek educational experiences that help us understand the central role of culture. We must create opportunities to critique the current educational system and strive toward developing as master teachers whose goal is to provide anti-bias and culturally relevant educational experiences for all children.

Figure 5.1.

I hope that this chapter has not only introduced the primary components of anti-bias education and culturally relevant education but also has helped you to consider why this work is important and how you can use your power and privilege as an early childhood professional to make our world, educational opportunities, and child outcomes more just and equitable.

Thirty years ago, Louise Derman-Sparks proclaimed that we needed anti-bias education in our world today, starting with our youngest citizens. The word cloud provides a visual of the –isms we face in America and speaks to the many issues of justice and equity that we still have to address. Children are intellectually capable of internalizing complex societal issues, stereotypes, and prejudices. They observe how we react (or don't) when we talk about the latest debate on immigration reform. They hear us champion or dismiss the Black Lives Matter movement. They take in the messages behind "Make America Great Again" and our reactions to these messages. Therefore, I ask you to consider how you can first position yourself within the larger society by rejecting biases and prejudices and speaking out against them.

I also encourage you to be your own advocate and promoter of anti-bias and culturally relevant education by conducting action research or inviting researchers into your classroom to examine how anti-bias education and CRP is helping to transform teaching, learning, and equitable experiences and outcomes for the children and families you serve. Use your success and learning experiences from implementing anti-bias education and CRP to help address educational policies at the classroom, program, local, and state levels when these policies do not support a culturally affirming and anti-bias education for young children. The lights and cameras are now on you. How will you use this spotlight and opportunity to make our world and early childhood field better?

Reflection Questions

> Do you feel equipped for and/or comfortable with teaching in an anti-bias and culturally relevant manner?

> What resources will you require to provide culturally relevant and anti-bias teaching in your classroom?

> Have you examined your own biases, prejudices, and stereotyping?

> How does your classroom environment represent anti-bias teaching? (For example, do you display and use posters, signs, photographs, dramatic play materials, and language that authentically represent the diversity of children and families you serve?)

> How do your interactions with young children build upon the culture and language they bring with them to the classroom?

> What is your knowledge about the cultural experiences and funds of knowledge of the children and families you serve?

CHAPTER 6:

IN A LANGUAGE OF THEIR OWN: AN OBSERVATIONAL TOOL TO CAPTURE YOUNG CHILDREN'S RACIAL ATTITUDES

» KERRY-ANN ESCAYG, PHD

Debi, the researcher, is watching the children play outside from a strategic place. There are two children at play with shovels and buckets in the sandbox a few feet away from her. As they both play, Brittany, a three-year-old White child, informs Taleshia, a Black child, "You're the same color as the rabbit poop." Taleshia stares at Brittany and frowns deeply. Brittany picks up a rabbit pellet from the sand, holds it up close to Taleshia's arm, and says, "See?" She smiles at Taleshia. "Your skin is shitty!" Brittany smiles triumphantly. "You have to leave. We don't allow shit in the sandbox." Taleshia stares at Brittany for a quiet moment then slaps Brittany's hand away, retorting, "Shut up!" She leaves the sandbox. (Van Ausdale and Feagin, 2001)

The preceding excerpt was taken from an ethnographic study on children and race. Depending on your background knowledge of children, race, and racism, the narrative might startle you. You might even interpret the episode with the same emotions as Taleshia: anger and hurt. However, what we cannot ignore is that Brittany associated Taleshia's dark skin color with something that is undesirable and then used this association to exclude Taleshia from the play activity. Also important is how Taleshia reacts to the comment. She frowns deeply. The comment wounds the child. She retaliates in anger. If you were a witness to this event, how would you respond?

Addressing children's knowledge of race remains key to implementing anti-bias/anti-racist teaching practice. Yet, many educators firmly believe in the concept of children's "racial innocence." Generally, teachers express this perspective by saying, "Children do not see race or color; they just see people." Many research studies have shown otherwise. Children do see race. Children do ascribe negative and positive meanings to racial groups, and White children in particular often use their beginning understandings of White privilege to wound and exclude.

At this point, pause and consider: What are your thoughts about children and race? Do you believe they are racially innocent? How would this view affect your approach to anti-bias teaching?

Drawing on data from the studies on children and race, this chapter provides an observational tool that captures salient findings on children's racial attitudes. Each category of the observation tool represents a central research finding. You can use this tool to identify what children understand about race and how they might be enacting racial systems of power and status through their play activities.

One caveat, however: To use such a tool effectively, you must first engage in critical self-reflection of your own socialization experiences and implicit racial bias. If not, you will fail to detect and interpret the meanings of children's comprehension of race as well as their behaviors through which they are enacting racist incidents (see, for example, Van Ausdale and Feagin, 2001). The observation measure is part of an ongoing teaching process of social and personal reflection. The questions at the end of this chapter are a starting point. However, you should read additional sources on racism and seek the relevant professional training opportunities, as these will encourage you to rethink your own experiences and or perceptions. Such activities will engage you, the educator, in critical self-reflection while also increasing your awareness and understanding of racial oppression, including how both color-blindness and anti-Blackness support White racial domination in the United States (Escayg, 2018). Simply stated, by identifying and disrupting perceptions concerning children, race, and racism, you can create authentic anti-racist classroom spaces in which children of color can thrive academically and develop pride in their racial and cultural identities. Additionally, anti-racist teaching practices—such as teaching activities focused on examining the nature and root of racism, racial inequalities, stereotypes, and White privilege—can provide young White children with accurate knowledge regarding racism, expose them to alternative narratives, foster perspective-taking skills, and contribute to the early development of an anti-racist White identity.

A HISTORICAL AND CONTEMPORARY REVIEW OF CHILDREN AND RACE

To grasp the findings of the research on children and race, some definitions are needed. *Racial awareness*, as the name implies, refers to children's recognition of skin color and hair texture, while *racial self-identification* involves children assigning a particular racial label to themselves and/or identifying based on skin color

(Aboud, 1987; Swanson et al., 2009). Ample empirical evidence has shown that the preschool age range (three to five years old) marks the onset of all dimensions of children's racial identity development, including self-identification.

Racial awareness: recognition of skin color and hair texture

Researchers have assessed children's racial self-identification using perceived-similarity tasks as well as short, semistructured interviews. Specifically, the investigator presents photos or dolls (see, for example, the doll-test study in Clark and Clark, 1947) depicting White children and children of color as well as adults and asks the child to select the photo or doll that looks most like him. Additional procedures involve posing questions such as, "Are you White?" or "Are you Black?" (In older studies, scholars used the terms *Negro* or *colored* instead of *Black*.) The goal is to determine whether the child will identify with his racial group. Some of the earlier studies found that while African American children did not identify with their racial group (either through selecting a doll or photo or with racial labels), White children accurately self-identified, regardless of the measures used (see, for example, Morland, 1963; Stevenson and Stewart, 1958).

Racial self-identification: assigning a particular racial label to oneself and/or identifying based on skin color

Over the years, however, contrasting data have emerged as researchers investigating children and race in international contexts have discovered that not all African American and Black children reject their racial identity but instead accurately identify with their own racial group (Davis, Leman, and Barrett, 2007; Fox and Jordan, 1973; Gregor and McPherson, 1966; Hraba and Grant, 1970; Jordan and Hernandez-Reif, 2009). Scholars have also advised that the misidentification among Black children, along with a pro-White racial preference, should not be interpreted as indicative of low self-esteem (Swanson et al., 2009). Self-concept and racial attitudes are two separate constructs; these constructs were not assessed independently of each other in previous studies.

Perceived similarity: a task used by researchers to assess self-identification based on similar characteristics such as skin color

Researchers have also assessed children's racial attitudes. According to Rotheram and Phinney (1987), researchers investigate children's racial attitudes by assessing "children's preferences or liking for their own or another ethnic group and their negative attitudes toward other groups." Negative attitudes toward other groups have also been described as *prejudice* (Aboud, 1988), as both involve negative evaluations of a particular racial or ethnic group. To assess children's racial prejudice—that is, the attributes they assign to majority and minority groups—many of the early studies (Bagley and Young, 1988; Branch and Newcombe, 1986; Clark and Clark, 1947; Doyle and Aboud, 1995; Semaj, 1980) employed dolls, the Preschool Racial Attitude Measure (PRAM II) (Williams et al., 1975), and the Multiresponse Racial Attitude Measure (Doyle and Aboud, 1995).

While both measures require children to assign positive traits, such as *healthy, good,* and *nice,* and negative traits, such as *bad, mean,* and *dirty,* to photos depicting White and Black children, the Multiresponse Racial Attitude Measure allows children to select more than one photo in response to the scenario provided. The materials for the Multiresponse Racial Attitude Measure include cards that contain a visual of the positive and negative adjectives and boxes that are "labeled as belonging to a White child, a Black child, and a Native Indian child" (Aboud, 2003). Each box has a picture depicting both race and gender (for example, a Black girl and a Black boy). The researcher then provides the child with three cards, and instructs the child "to place them in the box or boxes of people who are that way." One question reads: "Some children are naughty. They often do things like drawing on the wall with crayons. Who is naughty? Is it the Black child, the White child, the Indian child, or more than one child who is naughty?" These measures generally assess explicit racial attitudes; in recent years, however, researchers have assessed children's implicit racial attitudes (see, for example, Williams and Steele, 2019).

Findings from the large body of literature on children and prejudice, whether derived from the PRAM II, the doll test, or the Multiresponse Racial Attitude Measure, indicate that as early as three years of age (but declining after the age of seven) White children not only evaluate their own group positively but also exhibit negative racial attitudes toward members of other groups (for review, see Raabe and Beelmann, 2011). By contrast, minority children—and Black children in particular—before the age of seven demonstrate a pro-White bias. Age-related shifts have been reported, however. Specifically, beginning around the age of seven, Black children demonstrate more pro-Black attitudes (Aboud and Amato, 2001). While there are several explanations for the pattern of White preference and positive evaluations among both White and minority children during the preschool years, a fundamental question persists: Why are pro-bias attitudes so prominent in both minority and White children?

One explanation is that age-related cognitive limitations make young children susceptible to judging others based on external and not internal criteria (Aboud, 2008; Aboud and Amato, 2001); in other words, very young children are not cognitively ready to look beyond visible physical traits as they categorize people. However, the Hagerman study (2016) shows that among older White children, racial bias persists. Qualitative research attends to these inconsistencies by clarifying how children "do or live race" in early childhood contexts (Van Ausdale and Feagin, 1996; 2001). These findings revealed White children's ability to recognize—and rework—the specific privileges associated with their White identity, including its power and social status. That is, while White children may not be able to discuss it in detail, they are able to note that being White is preferred to being non-White.

> While White children may not be able to discuss it in detail, they are able to note that being White is preferred to being non-White.

ETHNOGRAPHIC DATA REVIEW

Although comparably a smaller body of literature, observations of young children in early childhood settings and elementary schools have provided multilayered insights into the ways in which minority and White children interpret, rework, and demonstrate context-specific racial beliefs. In previous investigations, particularly in the United Kingdom and the United States, researchers found that the societal context, and how racism functions in such a context, influenced children's play activities (Keys Adair and Doucet, 2014). Contemporary studies have used similar procedures. For instance, in addition to using self-portraiture, portraiture, ethnographic feedback, child interviews, and stories with dolls, MacNaughton,

Davis, and Smith (2009) employed observations over the course of eighteen months to explore how young children (three to five years of age) in four Australian early childhood settings enacted and performed their understanding of race. One of the most salient findings that emerged was a pattern of exclusion based on race.

The authors noted that "children from non-dominant racial backgrounds were actively excluded by children from the dominant racial backgrounds." Furthermore, teachers were unaware that race—and children's racial knowledge—played a significant role in structuring children's play interactions (MacNaughton, Davis, and Smith, 2009). From an analytical perspective, however, it can be argued that the practice of excluding minority children from play or peer interactions signifies dominant-group/White young children's awareness of the positive value ascribed to their group membership. This analysis may diverge from the age-stage–based interpretations of children's racial attitudes; nevertheless, this analysis agrees with anti-racist and critical race scholarship that highlights and looks at how White privilege functions in the wider society and in educational contexts (Kendall, 2013; Ladson-Billings and Tate, 2017; Rector-Aranda, 2016).

RACE AND INTERSECTIONALITY IN CHILDREN'S LIVES: WHAT TO LOOK FOR

Investigations that have used observations, instead of psychological testing and measures, to assess children's racial attitudes tend to be either structured or unstructured. While each has specific advantages, the structured observation tool contains preset specific items related to the research questions guiding the investigation (Phellas, Bloch, and Seale, 2012). That is, the researcher focuses on specific behaviors that can generate data consistent with the goal of the study. MacNaughton, Davis, and Smith (2009) used such a method in their work on Australian children and race.

What is critical race theory?

In broad terms, critical race theory (CRT) is based on two common themes: that the law and power structures in the United States support and maintain White supremacy and racial power, and that it is possible to transform the relationships between law and power to create a more equitable structure. CRT looks at race not as a biological fact but as a social construct. "According to CRT, racial inequality emerges from the social, economic, and legal differences that White people create between 'races' to maintain elite White interest in labour markets and politics and as such create the circumstances that give rise to poverty and criminality in many minority communities" (Curry, 2018).

The observation tool included in this chapter is based on an anti-racist and critical race theory analysis of children's racial attitudes. In particular, the observation guidelines reflect Black Feminist thought as conceptualized by Collins (2000), intersectionality conceptualized by Crenshaw (1995), as well as areas of the children-and-race empirical and theoretical literature that, while central to theorizing anti-racism praxis in the early years, have been relatively underdeveloped and underexplored. *Intersectionality* refers to the idea that one particular social identity, such as race, cannot provide the full picture of how racism and oppression affect Black women. The writings of African American female scholars such as Kimberle Crenshaw and Patricia Hill Collins highlight and critique the double forms of oppression African American women face, because of their race and their gender.

You can use this observation tool to identify what children understand about race and how, through play, they might be acting out their preliminary understandings of the relationship between racial identity, power, and disadvantage. It is important to note, however, that each category and the corresponding items in the observation tool are not mutually exclusive. For instance, you can look at your observation notes on peer interactions along with your notes on the language children use to reveal data pertaining both to Whiteness and to the negative imagery and stereotypes of Blacks. The observation tool is informed by research conducted with children aged three to six. Therefore, it is more suitable for educators working in play-based environments, prekindergarten, kindergarten, and first grade. Another important caveat to mention is that the present instrument includes three main categories:

White privilege, anti-Blackness, and intersectionality. Instead of aiming to observe these categories all at once, devote a couple of weeks for each category. For teachers working in a predominantly White setting, the observations should focus on how children talk about other racial groups (*racial language*), how and if they use diverse learning materials (if such are available in the classroom), and how they discuss their own White identity.

WHITE PRIVILEGE

White children enact White privilege through excluding minority children and assigning positive racial evaluations to themselves and negative evaluations to people of color (see, for example, Ebrahim and Francis, 2008; MacNaughton, Davis, and Smith, 2009; Miller, 2015; Paley, 1979). Therefore, when you are observing incidents for this category, you should observe peer interactions. Look for the following:

> Specifically, who is being included?

> Specifically, who is being excluded?

> What reasons do children provide for these behaviors?

Pay attention to the language children use:

> How do children describe play materials that reflect different racial groups, such as a Black doll or a White doll?

> If a child is creating a self-portrait, how does the child describe the color she has selected?

Observing sociodramatic play can also provide you with rich and specific information about children's racial knowledge.

> Who play the roles that reflect a higher socioeconomic status?

> Who is excluded from playing such roles and by whom?

> Are minority children being excluded from any particular center?

> What is the content of the sociodramatic play?

> Do these types of play reflect current stereotypical representations of minority groups?

ANTI-BLACKNESS

Observing children's sociodramatic activities, such as which roles are assigned to Black boys and girls, can give you insight on how anti-Blackness is influencing children's social interactions. This is particularly important for teachers in an integrated setting. Consisting of socially constructed narratives and negative representations, along with oppressive social and institutional practices, *anti-Blackness* means that the Black body is viewed as inferior to the White body—and treated as such. Given the long-standing legacy of racism in the United States, children's play may reflect elements of anti-Blackness, including racial stereotypes and a bias or preference for lighter skin tones (see, for example, Adams, Kurtz-Costes, and Hoffman, 2016; Averhart and Bigler, 1997; Connolly, 1995; Feagin, 2014; Miller, 2015; Rizvi, 1993; Van Ausdale and Feagin, 1996; 2001).

To determine whether a White child has internalized anti-Blackness, and by extension, White superiority (as one gives rise to the other), you need to look for interactions in which a sense of entitlement is enacted.

> Is the White child consistently enforcing "authority" or control over the minority child—and expecting the minority child's deference?

> Is the White child using racial language to justify this type of behavior?

> Pay attention to how White and minority children talk about skin color. What descriptors (adjectives) do they use?

> When Black children draw a self-portrait, do they avoid using the appropriate marker/crayon?

Children also express anti-Blackness through interactions that signify either distancing from Black children or fear of Black children (see, for example, Miller, 2015; Van Ausdale and Feagin, 1996; 2001). To observe such behaviors, use the following questions:

> Do White children avoid Black children?

> Do White children express fear or discomfort when they are in the presence of Black children?

INTERSECTIONALITY

In addition to White privilege and anti-Blackness, you also should observe activities for both racial and gender attitudes (see, for example, Daniel and Daniel, 1998; Fishbein, Malone, and Stegelin, 2009; Paley, 1994). For instance, do Black girls prefer White girls as playmates? Also, do White children recognize and extend one of the *controlling images* (Collins, 2000) of Black women (that is, the "mammy") to young Black girls? The mammy character refers to the Black female domestic. It is important to note that such an image, owing to its historical roots in slavery, signifies both race and gender oppression.

One context in which to observe incidents of possible awareness of the "mammy" controlling image is sociodramatic play. When observing such play, especially in games involving "princess" characters, it is important to ask these questions:

> ➤ How do Black girls participate?

> ➤ Do Black girls assume the role of princess without hesitation?

> ➤ Are Black girls prohibited from assuming the princess role? If so, by whom?

> ➤ Do both White and Black girls play with Black dolls? If so, what is the content of the play?

> ➤ If Black girls are invited to play, what type of play is it? Who controls the play, creating the content and assigning roles?

> ➤ Are Black girls charged with "servant" roles, and are they expected to perform these roles by White children?

Observations of children's play can provide the research data from which to construct an anti-bias program specific to the children in your program. The depth and type of the children's racial attitudes may vary. However, it is important to note that while conducting the observation, it may also be helpful to ask specific questions of a young child to clarify the reasoning behind his or her behavior. For instance, if you notice that a White child has excluded others based on race (an expression of White privilege) and the child has used derogatory language or performed behaviors that mirror racial beliefs, you should construct interview questions that will allow the child to speak more in depth about the deeper meanings behind those behaviors. Indeed, posing specific questions to the child regarding the incident observed can provide a more comprehensive account of the child's racial knowledge and assist you in developing focused anti-racist interventions. For example, ask preliminary questions such as the following:

> Can you tell me why you do not want to play with (insert child's name)?
> Can you tell me what (derogatory language about a child's racial group) means? Why did you say that word?

While interviewing the child can further sharpen the analysis of the data and guide your anti-bias/anti-racist efforts accordingly, contextualizing the behaviors within an anti-racist analysis may help you develop more nuanced interpretations. When teachers are trained to critically analyze children's play by drawing on an anti-racist perspective, as one study notes, "they realized that racism was part of the children's everyday play . . . [and] . . . decided to challenge the violence inherent in colonialism and the operation of power that created racialized and colonial hierarchies in the classroom" (Pacini-Ketchabaw, 2014).

In addition to completing the self-reflection exercise contained at the end of this chapter, observing students in the classroom with the criteria provided presents an opportunity not only to center the child and his racial knowledge, but also to use such awareness along with the research literature to create a broad spectrum of anti-racist learning activities tailored to individual and collective socio-emotional needs. For instance, if many of the children show behaviors reflective of the anti-Blackness discourse or feelings of White superiority, the anti-racist implications of such behaviors point to a need for discussions about racism, White privilege, and power. When discussing racism with young children, it is important for you to critique stereotypes and explain how negative images stem from unequal power relationships (see, for example, Escayg, 2019). You should also explore critical features of institutional racism, such as a lack of representation of people of color in key leadership positions.

More concrete applications entail an African-centered education, one that involves affirming physical characteristics, such as skin color and hair texture; including in the curriculum the contributions, culture, and histories of the African diaspora; and facilitating an understanding of and appreciation for pan-African identity (Boutte et al., 2017; Escayg, 2018; Powell-Hopson and Hopson, 1988; Shockley and Frederick, 2010). One way to promote an Afrocentric education, especially in the early years, is to ensure an Afrocentric learning environment. This will involve providing materials and learning opportunities such as the following:

> Children's books from Black authors

> Playdough, crayons, and markers in multicultural colors

> Music centers that include the instruments of the African diaspora, such as the steel pan, drum, and so on

> Clothing, such as the Ghanaian dashiki and kuka and the Nigerian iro, buba, and gele

> Ample opportunities for children to engage in storytelling!

Storytelling is one of the cultural traditions of African culture and can still be seen today in many of the diaspora cultures, including the Caribbean (Escayg and Kinkead-Clark, 2018).

Exposing young Black children to Afrocentric education fosters a positive Black identity. Escayg and Kinkead-Clark (2018), drawing on an anti-colonial Caribbean perspective, conceptualized a similar approach in their work on Caribbean early childhood education. Taken together, African-centered teaching combined with parental practices such as talking to children about their African American culture and history, challenges the defining characteristics of the anti-Blackness discourse and equips children with agency, self-love, and acceptance.

In sum, racism impacts a young child's sense of self. Anti-bias and anti-racist curricula and teaching activities (Escayg, 2018; Kissinger, 2017; LeeKeenan and Nimmo, 2016), while pedagogical interventions, also signify an act of love toward children and humanity: an act that, while discounted and eschewed by some, abides in hope, persists in adversity, and ultimately yields eternal rewards—for children and society.

Reflection Questions

> What is race?

> What is the difference between prejudice or bias and racism?

> Why is the concept of "children's racial innocence" so popular among early childhood educators?

> Evaluate your classroom centers and/or curriculum; do any of these reflect White privilege or anti-Blackness? How so? If not, why not?

> What is anti-bias and anti-racist early childhood education? How do these differ? How are they similar?

> How can you teach from an anti-racist perspective?

CHAPTER 7:

ANTI-BIAS SOCIAL JUSTICE EDUCATION: OUTSIDE THE CLASSROOM

This chapter will focus on how educators can help families become advocates for themselves. This will mean examining how to build an effective home-school-community partnership and collaboration by acknowledging past and current insults and also seeking to dismantle inequities to ensure that children are provided with equitable opportunities to learn.

Children spend the majority of their time, when not at home, in a school or classroom or another out-of-home program. Data from the US Department of Education National Household Education Survey shows that 47 percent of children under age one are in some out-of-home care setting, including center-based and home-based settings with relatives or nonrelatives (Corcoran, Steinley, and Grady, 2019). By the time children are five years old, almost three out of four of them (73 percent) are in at least one out-of-home care setting every week. This means that children learn a lot of who they are and what they should do and think from these settings. We often hear people talk fondly about their child-care teacher or third-grade teacher by saying things like, "Ms. Smith motivated me to do ____ and be ____" (you fill in the blanks). We also know that parents set the foundation for children's view of the world and how they carry themselves. This means that to set the foundation for children's school and life success, parents and child-care teachers and providers must be on the same page and must connect.

WHAT IS FAMILY ENGAGEMENT?

Family engagement used to be called *family involvement,* which focused on how much parents were involved in the caring and teaching of their child at home or school. However, many saw this terminology as a one-way street where programs and schools told parents what to do rather than developing a relationship built on respect. Now we are calling it *family engagement* as a way to ensure that it is not just about telling parents what to do but also helping programs and schools to do more to support families. This could include providing more resources for families, having more events that support families, and providing professional development to teachers and program and school staff to better work with and support families. Regardless of what we call family engagement, it is important that programs, schools, teachers, and staff define what they mean by family engagement; there are many ways to do so. We present a few in Table 7.1.

Table 7.1. Family Engagement Frameworks

Epstein's Six Types of Parent Involvement	
	1. **Parenting:** focused on helping families establish a home environment to support children's learning
	2. **Communicating:** focused on designing and implementing effective forms of school-home communication about school programs and children's progress
	3. **Volunteering:** focused on recruiting and organizing parents to help and support the school and classroom
	4. **Learning at home:** focused on providing information and ideas to families about how to help children with curriculum-related activities, such as homework
	5. **Decision making:** focused on including families as decision makers for school operations
	6. **Collaborating with community:** focused on coordinating resources and services from the community for the school, families, and children

Head Start's Parent-Family-Community Engagement Framework (US Department of Health and Human Services, 2011)	> Family well-being > Positive parent-child relationships > Families as lifelong educators > Families as learners > Family engagement in transitions > Family connections to peers and community > Families as advocates and leaders
Family Involvement (Fantuzzo, Tighe, and Childs, 2000)	> Home-based involvement > School-based involvement > Home-school conferencing
"Joining Together to Create a Bold Vision for Next Generation Family Engagement" (Weiss, Lopez, and Caspe, 2018)	> **Attendance:** focus on children's engagement in schools/programs > **Data sharing:** accessible, understandable, and actionable information about their children's progress and performance > **Academic and social development:** strategies that focus on content areas to allow families to play crucial and multiple roles in their children's education > **Digital media:** multiple opportunities to learn and engage with children and schools in different and connected ways > **Transitions:** focus on supporting families during key transition points, such as starting kindergarten, entering third grade, moving into middle and high school, and going to college, including extended learning opportunities such as after-school, clubs, and other learning contexts

As written by Iruka, Curenton, and Eke in their 2014 book *The CRAF-E4 Family Engagement Model: Building Practitioners' Competence to Work with Diverse Families*, these family engagement frameworks share many traits that are critically important in engaging with families—especially minority and immigrant families—and including low-income families. The authors address four key things, called the 4Es, that every early childhood professional and programs should do, especially when working with diverse families with a focus on supporting children's learning and development: exploration, expectation, education, and equipment.

THE 4Es

1. **Exploration:** Before early childhood professionals can effectively engage children and support their learning, they must first understand their families, including their goals and expectations. Research indicates that when families' goals and expectations are different from a school's, children will be confused and not feel connected to the learning. It is important that education professionals learn about children and families and their lived experiences, including goals focused on areas of strengths and areas that need strengthening.

2. **Expectation:** Having high expectations is one of the key strategies to supporting minority children and children from low-income households, especially Black children. Why would this not also be a key strategy for supporting and engaging with children's families, especially Black families and other families of color? Families of color, especially Black families, have a historical experience with education and schooling that has not always been positive. (Imagine the slurs being hurled at you when you are walking into a school that is Whites only.) Even for families who have had positive experiences, they still have concerns about how their child will be treated and how their perspectives will be addressed. They need to feel that their perspectives are not handled in a way that makes them feel "less than" or like second-class citizens. The family-engagement frameworks mentioned in Table 7.1 stress the importance of viewing parents as leaders and decision makers in the school. For parents to be decision makers and completely committed to the well-being of the school, staff, teachers, and learning community, they must have opportunities to engage in various aspects of school functioning, from small events to operational decisions such as curriculum, wrap-around services, hiring, and community engagement. It should be expected that parents, regardless of their economic standing, race, culture, or marital status, will be engaged. The voices of parents, especially those who are often not thought of, should be explicitly sought out and requested, because you expect them to be engaged. Parents live up to the expectations you have for them. If you have none, then they will likely not respond in the ways you hope they will.

3. Education: An early childhood program or school is usually the first institutional door that many families enter, other than the hospital or the doctor's office. While we often think of preschool as a transition for children, it is also often a transition for parents, especially for young parents, first-time parents, and non–English-speaking and immigrant families. While it is important to understand about families' goals (Exploration) and to require parental investment and engagement (Expectation), it is also important that early learning programs and schools serve as a place for becoming more knowledgeable about the education system from preschool to kindergarten and beyond. It is paramount that families understand the value of early learning and the importance of the early years for their child's school and life success. This will ensure that early learning continues to be as important as public education and that teachers and early education professionals are valued and paid fairly. When families understand the importance of child development and the early years, then they are likely to advocate that the school system take a pro-child-development, individualized approach for their child. Early care and education can be a source for combatting myths about K–12, about parental rights regarding special needs or gifted programs, and about how best to get support and assistance for various needs, such as mental-health services, substance-abuse programs, English-as-a-second-language classes, housing, and so on. This does not mean that teachers have to know every social-service program, but they must know the needs of their families and how to connect families with resources. This may mean creating a policy council, as seen with Head Start, or creating informal parenting groups where parents can lean on each other for information. This can be developed in the school or can be established in the virtual space through social media or Google groups.

4. Equipment: Regardless of which family-engagement framework guides your approach, the ultimate goal is that parents be equipped. While we often use the word *empowerment* when talking about family engagement, that term assumes that parents, especially those of color, don't have any power. Consequently, it is courageous of institutions to give power to "these people." This is not a strengths-based approach and undermines the power of family engagement. Rather than focusing on empowering families, the role of family engagement should focus on equipping families with the knowledge and practices about the education system and resources that can help them navigate and advocate on behalf of their children. Equipping families is particularly critical for marginalized families, especially poor families and families of color, whose concerns are often ignored.

Equipping families might take the forms of helping them navigate how to speak with their child's school about specific matters pertaining to their child, identifying school processes and procedures to support their child, and serving as a bridge to help families navigate the educational system. Equipping families with a network of other families would also be helpful, as many families are either facing or have faced similar questions. Equipping families can take many forms, but the goal is ensuring that families have what they need to support their child's learning and advocate for and support not only their own child but also other children.

THE 4Es IN ACTION

EXPLORATION

Consider Darnella Philippé, a Haitian parent whom you never see at drop-off. She has her cousin pick up her child. Do you see this parent as uninvolved or as hardworking? Do you know that the reason this parent may not be able to do drop-off is that her other child has to go to a particular program on the other side of town and because her husband works the third shift and doesn't get home in time to drop the child off? Do you know that this parent is trying to get her nursing degree and has classes during pickup? She calls on her cousin, whom she sees as a sister, to help with some of the household duties. These questions can only be answered through developing a relationship, having authentic communications with the parents, and keeping the child a central part of the conversation.

Questions for Discussion

> How do we engage these parents and their cousin as a family system?

> How do we inquire about how best to engage this family without asking them to participate in a way that we expect?

> How do we check our assumptions that this family is not engaged and does not care?

> How do we find out their goals for their child and what they are doing to support their child's learning?

EXPECTATION

Quintania, 35, is a human resource specialist for a travel firm. She has two children, four-year-old Dashon and seven-year-old Samantha, and is currently separated from her husband. Her two children go to two different schools, so she is often hustling to pick them up from their after-school programs, prepare dinner, help them finish homework, and get them ready for bed. She also has a part-time job as a bill coder, which she can do from her home at night. She has not attended any school events and really does not have time to attend any events, meetings, or even to volunteer due to her jobs and other commitments.

Questions for Discussion

> What expectations do you have for families?

> Why do you have those expectations? How do they matter for the school, classroom, and children? Have you talked with parents to confirm that these expectations are realistic and important?

> Have you talked with colleagues to confirm that these expectations are realistic and important?

> How do parents know about these expectations, beyond a list in the parent handbook?

> What are the different ways that parents can meet these expectations?

> What expectations do families have for you, and how do you know?

> Are there specific ways of engaging that you see as more valuable than others? For example, do you expect reading to the classroom, supporting teacher requests, buying supplies, attending school functions, being part of the parent-teacher organization/association? Why?

> Are there particular families who engage in certain activities?

> Are there other ways to ensure that all parents are able to meet the expectations without privileging those who have flexible schedules, work nine to five, are married or have a partner, are middle-class, and speak English?

> Since Quintania works from home for her part-time job, can we send her a short survey to see if there are things she needs to support her children?

> While she doesn't have the flexibility to come to the school for events, are there ways we can ask Quintania to tell us about her work, her role, and what she enjoys most about them? Can we share this with other parents?

> How can we go about engaging with Quintania's husband and the father of the children?

EDUCATION

Think of Darnella Philippé, our parent who was mentioned earlier. What would you think if you learned that part of her challenge with doing drop-off and pickup is her lack of access to reliable transportation? They have only one car, which her husband needs to go to work. The option to drop her husband off at work with the children at midnight did not work out well in the past because the children did not get enough sleep and did not function well the next day.

Questions for Discussion

> What if transportation was a major issue for most families in your classroom and this was the reason many children were absent?

> What if transportation was an issue for one child who happens to be a child of color? Do you believe it is the fault of the parents?

> What do you see as your role in helping families navigate these life challenges?

> What about the parent who has limited English and really needs information about getting help for his son to get an Individualized Education Plan?

> How do you gather needs assessment from families?

> How often do you gather this information?

> What do you do with this information?

> How do you ensure that families are getting the information they need?

EQUIPMENT

John, 36, is a hospital supervisor who trains all incoming nurses. He has been a widower for one year and is the father of three children under age five. He feels very uncomfortable in approaching his children's teachers because of his height (he is 6 feet 5 inches tall) and deep voice, which he has heard can be intimidating to many people. John is very active at home with his kids, playing with them and having conversations about many subjects, from how to behave in public to the solar system. He has been curious about learning more about how the school and teachers are ensuring that his children are being pushed, encouraged, and challenged. He doesn't know what assessments are used to ensure that his children are on grade level. He is also beginning to think about what school would work best for his three children, as one seems very gifted, another is still having some challenges with reading, and the other seems musically inclined. He is unclear whether any of his children should be tested and how he can go about finding out more.

Questions for Discussion

> Do you think it is your role to educate families about the education system? If not, whose role should it be?

> What are the ways you equip families with knowledge about education or early childhood?

> What is your response when families come to you about how to select a school for their child or children?

> How do you help families access supports for themselves or their child? In the case of John, how do we support his role as a single father who recently lost his wife?

> How do you know when you have equipped parents to support or advocate for their child?

> Are there systems you or your program/school have in place to ensure that families can call on each other or use each other as a resource?

> Early education programs and schools seem more comfortable for women and mothers. What can be done to create a culture that welcomes men and fathers, as well as different types of families?

LINKING FAMILY ENGAGEMENT FRAMEWORKS TO EQUITY AND SOCIAL JUSTICE

You may have heard the proverb, "Give a man a fish, and you feed him for a day. Teach a man to fish, and you feed him for a lifetime." While the ultimate goal of family engagement is to support the learning and development of children, it is important that early childhood leaders and practitioners see engagement as critical for social justice and equity.

Head Start began as an eight-week program focusing on children who were getting ready for kindergarten. The evidence shows that it is critical to prepare children for school and life by also connecting with their families and lived experiences (NASEM, 2016). (See the HighScope Perry Preschool and Carolina Abecedarian Study description in chapter 1. These programs included home visiting and parenting support as part of their projects.) The current structure of Head Start is one that focuses on both the child and the family, because educators and policy makers recognize that families matter for children's cognition, social, and emotional development and for their life success. Families are the consistent ones who are going to be there for children as they transition to school and life. More importantly, to ensure that the investment made in children continues through school and life, it is critical that parents are part of this journey and leverage the information, resources, and network they need. While we can focus on the short-term goal of getting children prepared for school, we must work toward the long-term goal of supporting and engaging with families, especially marginalized families, as the information shared will last a lifetime and be passed on for generations.

Family engagement is not about getting families into the school; it is about shaping the way that families operate to advocate for their own children, for other children, for other families, and for communities. If we strengthen the skill sets of families, we are improving the livelihood of a community. Think of the one parent who, through resources from the school, is able to get her degree and then access microlending to open a store, which becomes the place where the community congregates. It is a source of employment for others in the community. It is where young people get their first experience in working and developing soft skills. Thus, family engagement has the potential to be the way that we systematically address discrimination and bias, while also providing opportunities for all to thrive. This approach not only requires a commitment to the idea that every family matters but also acknowledges that some families have a higher mountain to climb and a longer road to walk.

> Firefighters oversee all the homes in a community. To ensure that the rest of the homes are not in danger, the firefighters must go to the burning home.

Educators must ensure that all children are getting what they need, but some children need specific supports and attention beyond the needs of some of their peers. Similarly, many families are doing well, but it is paramount that we ensure that all families are engaged and supported. In particular, it is critically important that we find, help, educate, inform, and equip families who need us the most. Equity is not equality.

Reflection Questions

> What steps do you take to learn about your families prior to school starting?

> What steps do you take to continue to learn about your families during the school year?

> How do you learn about parents' goals and expectations for their children?

> What expectations do you have of families?

> Do you think your expectations would be different if you were somewhere else? Why or why not?

> How do you educate families about your school and what you do with their children?

> How do you help families transition to pre-K or kindergarten?

> Do you share the same information with all the families, or do you tailor the information according to the families' needs? Why?

RESOURCES FOR INCREASING AND SUPPORTING FAMILY ENGAGEMENT

> *5 Benefits of Human-Centered Design Thinking for Family Engagement* by Margaret Caspe and Lorette McWilliams in collaboration with Early Learning Lab and National Center for Families Learning. https://globalfrp.org/content/download/509/4350/file/GFRP_HCD4FE.pdf

> *Human-Centered Design: An Innovative Tool for Professional Learning in Family Engagement* by the Global Family Research Project. https://globalfrp.org/content/download/295/3154/file/GFRP_Human-CenteredDesignGuide.pdf

> "Home Visiting and Early Childhood Education Can Benefit Families by Broadening Their Strategies for Family Engagement" by Manica F. Ramos and Sarah Shea Crowne. https://www.childtrends.org/home-visiting-early-childhood-education-benefit-families-broadening-strategies-family-engagement

> "Indicators of High-Quality Family Engagement in QRIS and Continuous Quality Improvement Systems: Connecting Research and Practice" address by Nancy Darlington and Manica Ramos. The QRIS Learning Network page includes links to useful related resources. https://qrisnetwork.org/member/calendar/event/190301/indicators-high-quality-family-engagement-qris-and-continuous-quality-i

> "Joining Together to Create a Bold Vision for Next-Generation Family Engagement: Engaging Families to Transform Education" by Heather B. Weiss, M. Elena Lopez, and Margaret Caspe. https://globalfrp.org/Articles/Joining-Together-to-Create-a-Bold-Vision-for-Next-Generation-Family-Engagement-Engaging-Families-to-Transform-Education

> *Opening Doors for Young Parents* by the Annie E. Casey Foundation. https://www.aecf.org/m/resourcedoc/aecf-openingdoorsforyoungparents-2018.pdf

REFERENCES AND RECOMMENDED READING

Aboud, Frances. 1987. "The Development of Ethnic Self-Identification and Attitudes." In *Children's Ethnic Socialization: Pluralism and Development*. Newbury Park, CA: SAGE.

Aboud, Frances. 1988. *Children and Prejudice*. Oxford, UK: Basil Blackwell.

Aboud, Frances. 2003. "The Formation of In-Group Favoritism and Out-Group Prejudice in Young Children: Are They Distinct Attitudes?" *Developmental Psychology* 39(1): 48–60.

Aboud, Frances. 2008. "A Social-Cognitive Developmental Theory of Prejudice." In *Handbook of Race, Racism, and the Developing Child*. Hoboken, NJ: John Wiley and Sons.

Aboud, Frances, and Maria Amato. 2001. "Developmental and Socialization Influences on Intergroup Bias." In *Blackwell Handbook of Social Psychology: Intergroup Processes*. Malden, MA: Blackwell.

Aboud, Frances, et al. 2012. "Interventions to Reduce Prejudice and Enhance Inclusion and Respect for Ethnic Differences in Early Childhood: A Systematic Review." *Developmental Review* 32(4): 307–336.

Adams, Elizabeth, Beth Kurtz-Costes, and Adam Hoffman. 2016. "Skin Tone Bias among African Americans: Antecedents and Consequences across the Life Span." *Developmental Review* 40: 93–116.

Administration for Children and Families. n.d. Head Start Timeline. US Department of Health and Human Services, Administration for Children and Families. https://eclkc.ohs.acf.hhs.gov/about-us/article/head-start-timeline

Annie E. Casey Foundation. 2018. *Opening Doors for Young Parents*. Baltimore, MD: Annie E. Casey Foundation. https://www.aecf.org/m/resourcedoc/aecf-openingdoorsforyoungparents-2018.pdf

Associated Press. 2017. "14 High-Profile Police-Related Deaths of U.S. Blacks." CBC, Dec. 7. https://www.cbc.ca/news/world/list-police-related-deaths-usa-1.4438618

Averhart, Cara, and Rebecca Bigler. 1997. "Shades of Meaning: Skin Tone, Racial Attitudes, and Constructive Memory in African American Children." *Journal of Experimental Child Psychology* 67(3): 363–388.

Bagley, Christopher, and Loretta Young. 1988. "Evaluation of Color and Ethnicity in Young Children in Jamaica, Ghana, England, and Canada." *International Journal of Intercultural Relations* 12(1): 45–60.

Banks, Antoine, and Heather Hicks. 2016. "Fear and Implicit Racism: Whites' Support for Voter ID Laws." *Political Psychology* 37(5): 641–658.

Barnett, W. Steven, Megan Carolan, and David Johns. 2013. *Equity and Excellence: African-American Children's Access to Quality Preschool.* http://nieer.org/wp-content/uploads/2016/08/Equity20and20Excellence20African-American20ChildrenE28099s20Access20to20Quality20Preschool_0.pdf

Birch, Sondra H., and Gary W. Ladd. 1998. "Children's Interpersonal Behaviors and the Teacher-Child Relationship." *Developmental Psychology* 34(5): 934–946.

Blake, Aaron. 2017. "Republicans' Views of Blacks' Intelligence, Work Ethic Lag Behind Democrats at a Record Clip." *The Washington Post.* March 31. https://www.washingtonpost.com/news/the-fix/wp/2017/03/31/the-gap-between-republicans-and-democrats-views-of-african-americans-just-hit-a-new-high/

Bobo, Lawrence. 2001. "Racial Attitudes and Relations at the Close of the Twentieth Century." In *America Becoming: Racial Trends and Their Consequences*, vol. 1. Washington, DC: National Academy Press.

Bobo, Lawrence, and Camille Charles. 2009. "Race in the American Mind: From the Moynihan Report to the Obama Candidacy." *The Annals of the American Academy of Political and Social Science* 621(1): 243–259.

Boehman, Joe. 1987. *Cultural Awareness Inventory.* Greenville, NC: East Carolina University. http://www.myacpa.org/sites/default/files/q%26s.pdf

Bonilla-Silva, Eduardo. 2010. *Racism without Racists: Color-Blind Racism and Racial Inequality in Contemporary America.* 3rd ed. Lanham, MD: Rowman and Littlefield.

Bosland, Julie, et al. 2011. "Educational Alignment to Promote Early Grade Success: Profiles of City Innovation." *National Civic Review* 100(4): 27–36.

Boutte, Gloria. 2012. "Urban Schools: Challenges and Possibilities for Early Childhood and Elementary Education." *Urban Education* 47(2): 515–550.

Boutte, Gloria. 2015. *Educating African American Students: And How Are the Children?* London, UK: Routledge.

Boutte, Gloria, et al. 2017. "Using African Diaspora Literacy to Heal and Restore the Souls of Young Black Children." *International Critical Childhood Policy Studies Journal* 6(1): 66–79.

Bowman, Phillip, and Cleopatra Howard. 1985. "Race-Related Socialization, Motivation, and Academic Achievement: A Study of Black Youths in Three-Generation Families." *Journal of the American Academy of Child and Adolescent Psychiatry* 24(2): 134–141.

Boysen, Guy A., and David L. Vogel. 2008. "The Relationship between Level of Training, Implicit Bias, and Multicultural Competency among Counselor Trainees." *Training and Education in Professional Psychology* 2(2): 103–110.

Branch, Curtis, and Nora Newcombe. 1986. "Racial Attitude Development among Young Black Children as a Function of Parental Attitudes: A Longitudinal and Cross-Sectional Study." *Child Development* 57(3): 712–721.

Braveman, Paula, et al. 2017. *What Is Health Equity? And What Difference Does a Definition Make?* Princeton, NJ: Robert Wood Johnson Foundation. https://www.rwjf.org/en/library/research/2017/05/what-is-health-equity-.html

Brophy, Jere, and Thomas Good. 1970. "Teachers' Communication of Differential Expectations for Children's Classroom Performance: Some Behavioral Data." *Journal of Educational Psychology* 61(5): 365–374.

Burchinal, Margaret, and Debby Cryer. 2003. "Diversity, Child Care Quality, and Developmental Outcomes." *Early Childhood Research Quarterly* 18(4): 401–426.

Campbell, Frances, et al. 2012. "Adult Outcomes as a Function of an Early Childhood Educational Program: An Abecedarian Project Follow-Up." *Developmental Psychology* 48(4): 1033–1043.

Carter, Dorinda. 2008. "Cultivating a Critical Race Consciousness for African American School Success." *Educational Foundations* 22(1–2): 11–28.

Carter, Samuel. 2000. *No Excuses: Lessons from Twenty-One High-Performing, High-Poverty Schools.* Washington, DC: Heritage Foundation.

Caspe, Margaret, and Lorette McWilliams. 2019. *5 Benefits of Human-Centered Design Thinking for Family Engagement.* In collaboration with Early Learning Lab and National Center for Families Learning. Global Family Research Project. https://globalfrp.org/content/download/509/4350/file/GFRP_HCD4FE.pdf

Castle, Billie, et al. 2019. "Public Health's Approach to Systemic Racism: A Systematic Literature Review." *Journal of Racial and Ethnic Health Disparities* 6(1): 27–36.

Centers for Disease Control and Prevention. n.d. "About the CDC–Kaiser Permanente ACE Study." Violence Prevention. Centers for Disease Control and Prevention. https://www.cdc.gov/violenceprevention/childabuseandneglect/acestudy/about.html

Clark, Kenneth, and Mamie Clark. 1947. "Racial Identification and Preference in Negro Children." In *Readings in Social Psychology.* New York, NY: H. Holt.

Cochran-Smith, Marilyn. 2004. "Defining the Outcomes of Teacher Education: What's Social Justice Got to Do with It?" *Asia-Pacific Journal of Teacher Education* 32(3): 193–212.

Cohn, D'Vera. 2016. "It's Official: Minority Babies Are the Majority among the Nation's Infants, but Only Just." Fact Tank. Pew Research Center. https://www.pewresearch.org/fact-tank/2016/06/23/its-official-minority-babies-are-the-majority-among-the-nations-infants-but-only-just/

Collins, Patricia Hill. 2000. *Black Feminist Thought: Knowledge, Consciousness, and the Politics of Empowerment.* New York, NY: Routledge.

Connolly, Paul. 1995. "Racism, Masculine Peer-Group Relations and the Schooling of African/Caribbean Infant Boys." *British Journal of Sociology of Education* 16(1): 75–92.

Conti, Gabriella, and James Heckman. n.d. "Early Childhood Development: Creating Healthy Communities with Greater Efficiency and Effectiveness." Investing in What Works for America's Communities. https://www.whatworksforamerica.org/ideas/early-childhood-development-creating-healthy-communities-with-greater-efficiency-and-effectiveness/

Corcoran, Lisa, Katrina Steinley, and Sarah Grady. 2019. *Early Childhood Program Participation, Results from the National Household Education Surveys Program of 2016: First Look.* Washington, DC: National Center for Education Statistics, Institute of Education Sciences, US Department of Education. https://nces.ed.gov/pubs2017/2017101REV.pdf

Correll, Joshua, et al. 2002. "The Police Officer's Dilemma: Using Ethnicity to Disambiguate Potentially Threatening Individuals." *Journal of Personality and Social Psychology* 83(6): 1314–1329.

Costello, Kimberly, and Gordon Hodson. 2014. "Explaining Dehumanization among Children: The Interspecies Model of Prejudice." *British Journal of Social Psychology* 53(1): 175–197.

Crenshaw, Kimberlé Williams. 1995. "Mapping the Margins: Intersectionality, Identity, Politics, and Violence Against Women of Color." In *Critical Race Theory: The Key Writings That Formed the Movement.* New York, NY: New Press.

Crosnoe, Robert, et al. 2010. "Instruction, Teacher-Student Relations, and Math Achievement Trajectories in Elementary School." *Journal of Educational Psychology* 102(2): 407–417.

Crowley, Jocelyn, and Stephanie Curenton. 2011. "Organizational Social Support and Parenting Challenges among Mothers of Color: The Case of Mocha Moms." *Family Relations* 60(1): 1–14.

Curenton, Stephanie, Jocelyn Crowley, and Dawne Mouzon. 2018. "Qualitative Descriptions of Middle-Class, African American Mothers' Child-Rearing Practices and Values." *Journal of Family Issues* 39(4): 868–895.

Curenton, Stephanie, and Iheoma Iruka. 2013. *Cultural Competence in Early Childhood Education*. San Diego, CA: Bridgepoint Education.

Curry, Tommy. 2018. "Critical Race Theory." *Encyclopaedia Britannica*. https://www. britannica.com/topic/critical-race-theory

Daniel, Jerlean, and Jack Daniel. 1998. "Preschool Children's Selection of Race-Related Personal Names." *Journal of Black Studies* 28(4): 471–490.

Darlington, Nancy, and Manica Ramos. 2019. "Indicators of High-Quality Family Engagement in QRIS and Continuous Quality Improvement Systems: Connecting Research and Practice." QRIS National Learning Network. https://qrisnetwork.org/member/calendar/event/190301/indicators-high-quality-family-engagement-qris-and-continuous-quality-i

Davis, Heather A. 2003. "Conceptualizing the Role and Influence of Student-Teacher Relationships on Children's Social and Cognitive Development." *Educational Psychologist* 38(4): 207–234.

Davis, Stephanie, Patrick Leman, and Martyn Barrett. 2007. "Children's Implicit and Explicit Ethnic Group Attitudes, Ethnic Group Identification, and Self-Esteem." *International Journal of Behavioral Development* 31(5): 514–525.

Dee, Thomas S. 2005. "A Teacher Like Me: Does Race, Ethnicity, or Gender Matter?" *American Economic Review* 95(2): 158–165.

Derman-Sparks, Louise. 1993. "Empowering Children to Create a Caring Culture in a World of Differences." *Childhood Education* 70(2): 66–71.

Derman-Sparks, Louise, and the ABC Task Force. 1989. *Anti-Bias Curriculum: Tools for Empowering Young Children*. Washington, DC: NAEYC.

Derman-Sparks, Louise, and Julie Olsen Edwards. 2010. *Anti-Bias Education for Young Children and Ourselves*. 2nd ed. Washington, DC: NAEYC.

Derman-Sparks, Louise, and Carol Brunson Phillips. 1997. *Teaching/Learning Anti-Racism: A Developmental Approach*. New York, NY: Teachers College Press.

Devine, Patricia, et al. 2002. "The Regulation of Explicit and Implicit Race Bias: The Role of Motivations to Respond without Prejudice." *Journal of Personality and Social Psychology* 82(5): 835–848.

Dolan-Reilly, Georgianna. 2013. "The Definition of Social Justice." Social Justice Solutions. http://www.socialjusticesolutions.org/2013/01/15/the-definition-of-social-justice/

Dovidio, John, and Samuel Gaertner. 2000. "Aversive Racism and Selection Decisions: 1989 and 1999." *Psychological Science* 11(4): 315–319.

Dovidio, John, and Samuel Gaertner. 2004. "Aversive Racism." In *Advances in Experimental Social Psychology*. London, UK: Elsevier Academic Press.

Dovidio, John, et al. 2004. "Contemporary Racial Bias: When Good People Do Bad Things." In *The Social Psychology of Good and Evil*. New York, NY: Guilford.

Dovidio, John, Kerry Kawakami, and Samuel Gaertner. 2000. "Reducing Contemporary Prejudice: Combating Explicit and Implicit Bias at the Individual and Intergroup Level." In *Reducing Prejudice and Discrimination*. Mahwah, NJ: Lawrence Erlbaum Associates.

Downey, Douglas, and Shana Pribesh. 2004. "When Race Matters: Teachers' Evaluations of Students' Classroom Behavior." *Sociology of Education* 77(4): 267–282.

Doyle, Anna Beth, and Frances Aboud. 1995. "A Longitudinal Study of White Children's Racial Prejudice as a Social-Cognitive Development." *Merrill-Palmer Quarterly* 41(2): 209–228.

Driscoll, Amy, and Nancy Nagel. 2008. *Early Childhood Education, Birth–8: The World of Children, Families and Educators*. 5th ed. Boston, MA: Pearson.

Durden, Tonia, Elsa Escalante, and Kimberly Blitch. 2014a. *Culture Matters—Strategies to Support Young Children's Social and Cultural Development*. (Guide for professionals.) Lincoln, NE: University of Nebraska–Lincoln Extension, Institute of Agriculture and Natural Resources. http://extensionpublications.unl.edu/assets/pdf/g2241.pdf

Durden, Tonia, Elsa Escalante, and Kimberly Blitch. 2014b. *Culture Matters—Strategies to Support Your Young Child's Social and Cultural Development*. (Guide for parents.) Lincoln, NE: University of Nebraska–Lincoln Extension, Institute of Agriculture and Natural Resources. http://extensionpublications.unl.edu/assets/pdf/g2242.pdf

Durden, Tonia, Elsa Escalante, and Kimberly Blitch. 2015. "Start with Us! Culturally Relevant Pedagogy in the Preschool Classroom." *Early Childhood Education Journal* 43(3): 223–232.

Ebrahim, H., and Dennis Francis. 2008. "You Said, 'Black Girl': Doing Difference in Early Childhood." *Africa Education Review* 5(2): 274–287.

Echterhoff, Gerald, E. Tory Higgins, and John Levine. 2009. "Shared Reality: Experiencing Commonality with Others' Inner States about the World." *Perspectives on Psychological Science* 4(5): 496–521.

Egalite, Anna, Brian Kisida, and Marcus Winters. 2015. "Representation in the Classroom: The Effect of Own-Race Teachers on Student Achievement." *Economics of Education Review* 45(C): 44–52.

Eligon, John. 2018. "Hate Crimes Increase for the Third Consecutive Year, F.B.I. Reports." *The New York Times*. November 14, A 21.

Epstein, Rebecca, Jamilia Blake, and Thalia González. 2017. *Girlhood Interrupted: The Erasure of Black Girls' Childhood*. Washington, DC: Center on Poverty and Equality, Georgetown Law. https://www.law.georgetown.edu/poverty-inequality-center/wp-content/uploads/sites/14/2017/08/girlhood-interrupted.pdf

Escayg, Kerry-Ann. 2017. "Race in the Life of an Indo-Trinidadian Child: Debunking the Myth of 'Racial Innocence.'" Childhood Explorer. https://www.childhoodexplorer.org/race-in-the-life/

Escayg, Kerry-Ann. 2018. "The Missing Links: Enhancing Anti-Bias Education with Anti-Racist Education." *Journal of Curriculum, Teaching, Learning, and Leadership in Education* 3(1): 15–20. https://digitalcommons.unomaha.edu/ctlle/vol3/iss1/4/

Escayg, Kerry-Ann. 2019. "'Who's Got the Power?' A Critical Examination of the Anti-Bias Curriculum." *International Journal of Child Care and Education Policy* 13(6). https://ijccep.springeropen.com/articles/10.1186/s40723-019-0062-9

Escayg, Kerry-Ann, Rachel Berman, and Natalie Royer. 2017. "Canadian Children and Race: Toward an Antiracism Analysis." *Journal of Childhood Studies* 42(2): 10–21.

Escayg, Kerry-Ann, and Zoyah Kinkead-Clark. 2018. "Mapping the Contours of Caribbean Early Childhood Education." *Global Education Review* 5(4): 236–253.

Fantuzzo, John, Erin Tighe, and Stephanie Childs. 2000. "Family Involvement Questionnaire: A Multivariate Assessment of Family Participation in Early Childhood Education." *Journal of Educational Psychology* 92(2): 367–376.

Farkas, George, Robert Grobe, Daniel Sheehan, and Yuan Shaun. 1990. "Cultural Resources and School Success: Gender, Ethnicity, and Poverty Groups within an Urban School District." *American Sociological Review* 55(1): 127–142.

Feagin, Joe. 2014. *Racist America: Roots, Current Realities, and Future Reparations*. 3rd ed. New York, NY: Routledge.

Felitti, Vincent, et al. 1998. "Relationship of Childhood Abuse and Household Dysfunction to Many of the Leading Causes of Death in Adults." *American Journal of Preventive Medicine* 14(4): 245–258.

Fishbein, Harold, D. Michael Malone, and Dolores Stegelin. 2009. "Playmate Preferences of Preschool Children Based on Race, Sex, and Perceived Physical Attractiveness." In *From Children to Red Hatters: Diverse Images and Issues of Play*, vol. 8 of Play and Culture Studies. Lanham, MD: University Press of America.

Ford, Donna, and J. John Harris III. 1997. "A Study of the Racial Identity and Achievement of Black Males and Females." *Roeper Review* 20(2): 105–110.

Fox, David, and Valerie Jordan. 1973. "Racial Preference and Identification of Black, American Chinese, and White Children." *Genetic Psychology Monographs* 88(2): 229–286.

Gaertner, Samuel, and John Dovidio. 1986. "The Aversive Form of Racism." In *Prejudice, Discrimination, and Racism*. San Diego, CA: Academic Press.

Galinsky, Adam, and Gordon Moskowitz. 2000. "Perspective-Taking: Decreasing Stereotype Expression, Stereotype Accessibility, and In-Group Favoritism." *Journal of Personality and Social Psychology* 78(4): 708–724.

Gardner-Neblett, Nicole, Elizabeth Pungello, and Iheoma Iruka. 2012. "Oral Narrative Skills: Implications for the Reading Development of African American Children." *Child Development Perspectives* 6(3): 218–224.

Gawronski, Bertram, Etienne LeBel, and Kurt Peters. 2007. "What Do Implicit Measures Tell Us?: Scrutinizing the Validity of Three Common Assumptions." *Perspectives on Psychological Science* 2(2): 181–193.

Gay, Geneva. 2000. *Culturally Responsive Teaching: Theory, Research, and Practice*. New York: Teachers College Press.

Gay, Geneva. 2002. "Preparing for Culturally Responsive Teaching." *Journal of Teacher Education* 53(2): 106–116.

Geiger, A. W. 2018. "America's Public School Teachers Are Far Less Racially and Ethnically Diverse Than Their Students." Fact Tank. Pew Research Center. https://www.pewresearch.org/fact-tank/2018/08/27/americas-public-school-teachers-are-far-less-racially-and-ethnically-diverse-than-their-students/

Gilliam, Walter, et al. 2016. *Do Early Educators' Implicit Biases Regarding Sex and Race Relate to Behavior Expectations and Recommendations of Preschool Expulsions and Suspensions?* Research study brief. New Haven, CT: Yale Child Study Center. https://medicine.yale.edu/childstudy/zigler/publications/Preschool%20Implicit%20Bias%20Policy%20Brief_final_9_26_276766_5379_v1.pdf

Gilliam, Walter, and Chin Reyes. 2018. "Teacher Decision Factors That Lead to Preschool Expulsion: Scale Development and Preliminary Validation of the Preschool Expulsion Risk Measure." *Infants and Young Children* 31(2): 93–108.

Glander, Mark. 2015. *Selected Statistics from the Public Elementary and Secondary Education Universe: School Year 2013–14*. Washington, DC: US Department of Education, National Center for Education Statistics.

Global Family Research Project. n.d. *Human-Centered Design: An Innovative Tool for Professional Learning in Family Engagement.* https://globalfrp.org/content/download/295/3154/file/GFRP_Human-CenteredDesignGuide.pdf

Goff, Phillip, et al. 2014. "The Essence of Innocence: Consequences of Dehumanizing Black Children." *Journal of Personality and Social Psychology* 106(4): 526–545.

Goldhaber, Dan, and Michael Hansen. 2010. "Race, Gender, and Teacher Testing: How Informative a Tool Is Teacher Licensure Testing?" *American Educational Research Journal* 47(1): 218–251.

Gonzalez-Mena, Janet. 2009. *Child, Family, and Community: Family-Centered Early Care and Education.* 5th ed. Upper Saddle River, NJ: Merrill Pearson.

Good, Thomas. 1981. "Teacher Expectations and Student Perceptions: A Decade of Research." *Educational Leadership* 38(5): 415–422.

Green, Alexander, et al. 2007. "Implicit Bias among Physicians and Its Prediction of Thrombolysis Decisions for Black and White Patients." *Journal of General Internal Medicine* 22(9): 1231–1238.

Greenwald, Anthony, et al. 2009. "Understanding and Using the Implicit Association Test: III. Meta-Analysis of Predictive Validity." *Journal of Personality and Social Psychology* 97(1): 17–41.

Greenwald, Anthony, et al. 2009. "Implicit Race Attitudes Predicted Vote in the 2008 US Presidential Election." *Analyses of Social Issues and Public Policy* 9(1): 241–253.

Gregor, A. James, and D. Angus McPherson. 1966. "Racial Attitudes among White and Negro Children in a Deep-South Standard Metropolitan Area." *The Journal of Social Psychology* 68(1): 95–106.

Gross, Terry. 2017. "A 'Forgotten History' of How the US Government Segregated America." NPR. https://www.npr.org/2017/05/03/526655831/a-forgotten-history-of-how-the-u-s-government-segregated-america

Hagerman, Margaret Ann. 2016. "Reproducing and Reworking Colorblind Racial Ideology: Acknowledging Children's Agency in the White Habitus." *Sociology of Race and Ethnicity* 2(1): 58–71.

Hammond, Zaretta. 2015. *Culturally Responsive Teaching and the Brain: Promoting Authentic Engagement and Rigor among Culturally and Linguistically Diverse Students.* Thousand Oaks, CA: Corwin.

Harris, Cheryl. 1993. "Whiteness as Property." *Harvard Law Review* 106(8): 1707–1791.

Harris, Richard, and Doris Forrester. 2003. "The Suburban Origins of Redlining: A Canadian Case Study, 1935–54." *Urban Studies* 40(13): 2661–2686.

Hathaway, Bill. 2016. "Implicit Bias May Help Explain High Preschool Expulsion Rates for Black Children." YaleNews. https://news.yale.edu/2016/09/27/implicit-bias-may-help-explain-high-preschool-expulsion-rates-black-children

Heckman, James, and Ganesh Karapakula. 2019. "Intergenerational and Intragenerational Externalities of the Perry Preschool Project." Working Paper 2019-033. Chicago, IL: University of Chicago, Department of Economics, Human Capital and Economic Opportunity Global Working Group.

Hilliard, Asa III. 2000. "'Race,' Identity, Hegemony, and Education: What Do We Need to Know Now?" In *Race and Education: The Roles of History and Society in Educating African American Students*. Boston, MA: Allyn and Bacon.

Hodas, Gordon. 2006. *Responding to Childhood Trauma: The Promise and Practice of Trauma Informed Care*. Harrisburg, PA: Pennsylvania Office of Mental Health and Substance Abuse Services. http://www.childrescuebill.org/VictimsOfAbuse/RespondingHodas.pdf

Hoffman, Lee, and Jennifer Sable. 2006. *Public Elementary and Secondary Students, Staff, Schools, and School Districts: School Year 2003–04*. Washington, DC: US Department of Education, National Center for Education Statistics. https://nces.ed.gov/pubs2006/2006307.pdf

Holmes IV, Oscar, Marilyn Whitman, Kim Campbell, and Diane Johnson. 2016. "Exploring the Social Identity Threat Response Framework." *Equality, Diversity, and Inclusion: An International Journal* 35(3): 205–220.

Howard, Tyrone. 2001. "Telling Their Side of the Story: African-American Students' Perceptions of Culturally Relevant Teaching." *The Urban Review* 33(2): 131–149.

Howard, Tyrone. 2003. "Culturally Relevant Pedagogy: Ingredients for Critical Teacher Reflection." *Theory into Practice* 42(3): 195–202.

Hraba, Joseph, and Geoffrey Grant. 1970. "Black Is Beautiful: A Reexamination of Racial Preference and Identification." *Journal of Personality and Social Psychology* 16(3): 398–402.

Hussar, William, and Tabitha Bailey. 2017. *Projections of Education Statistics to 2025*. 44th ed. Washington, DC: US Department of Education, National Center for Education Statistics.

Hyun, Eunsook, and J. Dan Marshall. 2003a. "Teachable-Moment-Oriented Curriculum Practice in Early Childhood Education." *Journal of Curriculum Studies* 35(1): 111–127.

Hyun, Eunsook, and J. Dan Marshall. 2003b. "Critical Inquiry into Emergent-Oriented Curriculum Practice." *Journal of Early Childhood Teacher Education* 24(1): 37–50.

Irizarry, Yasmiyn. 2015. "Selling Students Short: Racial Differences in Teachers' Evaluations of High, Average, and Low Performing Students." *Social Science Research* 52: 522–538.

Iruka, Iheoma, Stephanie Curenton, and Tonia Durden, eds. 2017. *African American Children in Early Childhood Education: Making the Case for Policy Investments in Families, Schools and Communities.* Bingley, UK: Emerald Publishing.

Iruka, Iheoma, Tonia Durden, and Portia Kennel. 2015. "Changing Faces: Parenting, Culture, and Child Learning and Development." *Zero to Three* 35(4): 10–18.

Irvine, Jacqueline. 1990. *Black Students and School Failure: Policies, Practices, and Prescriptions.* Westport, CT: Greenwood.

Jacoby-Senghor, Drew, Stacey Sinclair, and J. Nicole Shelton. 2016. "A Lesson in Bias: The Relationship between Implicit Racial Bias and Performance in Pedagogical Contexts." *Journal of Experimental Social Psychology* 63: 50–55.

Jian, Yang, Maribel Granja, and Heather Koball. 2017. *Basic Facts about Low-Income Children: Children under 18 Years, 2015.* New York, NY: National Center for Children in Poverty.

Jordan, Phillip, and Maria Hernandez-Reif. 2009. "Reexamination of young children's racial attitudes and skin tone preferences." *Journal of Black Psychology* 35(3): 388–403.

Kanter, Jonathan, et al. 2017. "A Preliminary Report on the Relationship between Microaggressions against Black People and Racism among White College Students." *Race and Social Problems* 9(4): 291–299.

Katz, Phyllis. 2003. "Racists or Tolerant Multiculturalists? How Do They Begin?" *American Psychologist* 58(11): 897–909.

Kawakami, Kerry, et al. 2000. "Just Say No (to Stereotyping): Effects of Training in the Negation of Stereotypic Associations on Stereotype Activation." *Journal of Personality and Social Psychology* 78(5): 871–888.

Kawakami, Kerry, John Dovidio, and Simone van Kamp. 2005. "Kicking the Habit: Effects of Nonstereotypic Association Training and Correction Processes on Hiring Decisions." *Journal of Experimental Social Psychology* 41(1): 68–75.

Kendall, Frances. 2013. *Understanding White Privilege: Creating Pathways to Authentic Relationships Across Race.* 2nd ed. New York, NY: Routledge.

Keys Adair, Jennifer, and Doucet Fabienne. 2014. "The Impact of Race and Culture on Play in Early Childhood Classrooms." In *The SAGE Handbook of Play and Learning in Early Childhood.* London, UK: SAGE.

Kim, Catherine. 2019. "A White Woman from Ohio Asked Gillibrand about White Privilege. Her Answer Was Spot On." Vox. https://www.vox.com/policy-and-politics/2019/7/12/20691717/white-working-class-kirsten-gillibrand-white-privilege-institutional-racism

Kissinger, Katie. 2017. *Anti-Bias Education in the Early Childhood Classroom: Hand in Hand, Step by Step.* New York, NY: Routledge.

Kohli, Rita. 2009. "Critical Race Reflections: Valuing the Experiences of Teachers of Color in Teacher Education." *Race, Ethnicity, and Education* 12(2): 235–251.

Kok, Car Mun, et al. 2015. *Say What?—Understanding, Identifying, and Addressing Microaggressions.* Lincoln, NE: University of Nebraska–Lincoln Extension.

Krikorian, Greg. 1996. "More Blacks Imprisoned Under '3 Strikes,' Study Says." *Los Angeles Times*, March 5. https://www.latimes.com/archives/la-xpm-1996-03-05-mn-43270-story.html

Ladd, Gary, Sondra Birch, and Eric Buhs. 1999. "Children's Social and Scholastic Lives in Kindergarten: Related Spheres of Influence?" *Child Development* 70(6): 1373–1400.

Ladson-Billings, Gloria. 1994. *The Dreamkeepers: Successful Teachers of African American Children.* San Francisco, CA: Jossey-Bass.

Ladson-Billings, Gloria. 2014. "Culturally Relevant Pedagogy 2.0: a.k.a. the Remix." *Harvard Educational Review* 84(1): 74–84.

Ladson-Billings, Gloria, and William Tate IV. 2017. "Toward a Critical Race Theory of Education." In *Critical Race Theory in Education: All God's Children Got a Song.* New York, NY: Routledge.

LeeKeenan, Debbie, and John Nimmo. 2016. "Anti-Bias Education in Challenging Times." *Exchange* 38(6): 66–69.

Legault, Lisa, et al. 2007. "On the Self-Regulation of Implicit and Explicit Prejudice: A Self-Determination Theory Perspective." *Personality and Social Psychology Bulletin* 33(5): 732–749.

Lockhart, P. R. 2018. "A White Neighbor Called Police on a Kid Mowing a Lawn. Later, They Called as He Played in a Yard." Vox. https://www.vox.com/identities/2018/7/2/17527382/reggie-fields-racial-profiling-911-police

MacNaughton, Glenda, Karina Davis, and Kylie Smith. 2009. "Exploring 'Race-Identities' with Young Children: Making Politics Visible." In *"Race" and Early Childhood Education: An International Approach to Identity, Politics, and Pedagogy.* New York, NY: Palgrave Macmillan.

Markus, Hazel Rose, and Shinobu Kitayama. 1998. "The Cultural Psychology of Personality." *Journal of Cross-Cultural Psychology* 29(1): 63–87.

McCall, Robert, Cynthia Evahn, and Lynn Kratzer. 1992. *High School Underachievers: What Do They Achieve as Adults?* Thousand Oaks, CA: SAGE.

McKown, Clark, and Rhona Weinstein. 2008. "Teacher Expectations, Classroom Context, and the Achievement Gap." *Journal of School Psychology* 46(3): 235–261.

Miller, Erin. 2015. "Discourses of Whiteness and Blackness: An Ethnographic Study of Three Young Children Learning to Be White." *Ethnography and Education* 10(2): 137–153.

Minervino, Jim. 2014. *Lessons from Research and the Classroom: Implementing High-Quality Pre-K That Makes a Difference for Young Children.* White paper. Seattle, WA: Bill and Melinda Gates Foundation. https://docs.gatesfoundation.org/documents/lessons%20from%20research%20and%20the%20Classroom_September%202014.pdf

Moore, Eddie Jr., Ali Michael, and Marguerite Penick-Parks, eds. 2017. *The Guide for White Women Who Teach Black Boys.* Thousand Oaks, CA: Corwin.

Morland, J. Kenneth. 1963. "Racial Self-Identification: A Study of Nursery School Children." *The American Catholic Sociological Review* 24(3): 231–242.

Mosley, Melissa, and Rebecca Rogers. 2011. "Inhabiting the 'Tragic Gap': Pre-Service Teachers Practicing Racial Literacy." *Teaching Education* 22(3): 303–324.

Murray, Carolyn B. 1996. "Estimating Achievement Performance: A Confirmation Bias." *Journal of Black Psychology* 22(1): 67–85.

Musu-Gillette, Lauren, et al. 2016. *Status and Trends in the Education of Racial and Ethnic Groups 2016.* Washington, DC: US Department of Education, National Center for Education Statistics. https://nces.ed.gov/pubs2016/2016007.pdf

National Academies of Sciences, Engineering, and Medicine. 2016. *Parenting Matters: Supporting Parents of Children Ages 0–8.* Washington, DC: National Academies Press.

National Academies of Sciences, Engineering, and Medicine. 2019. *Vibrant and Healthy Kids: Aligning Science, Practice, and Policy to Advance Health Equity.* Washington, DC: National Academies Press. https://www.nap.edu/read/25466/chapter/1

National Assessment of Educational Progress. 2017. "No Significant Change in Eighth-Grade Reading Scores for Most Student Groups Compared to 2015." NAEP Reading Report Card. https://www.nationsreportcard.gov/reading_2017/nation/gaps/?grade=8

National Association for the Education of Young Children. 2011. *Code of Ethical Conduct and Statement of Commitment.* Washington, DC: NAEYC. https://www.naeyc.org/sites/default/files/globally-shared/downloads/PDFs/resources/position-statements/Ethics%20Position%20Statement2011_09202013update.pdf

National Voices Project. 2016. *Report Topic: Conversation Compass Professional Development Culturally Responsive Teaching Practices*. Ann Arbor, MI: W.K. Kellogg Foundation.

Newheiser, Anna-Kaisa, and Kristina Olson. 2012. "White and Black American Children's Implicit Intergroup Bias." *Journal of Experimental Social Psychology* 48(1): 264–270.

NewsOne. 2019. "64 Black Men And Boys Killed By Police." NewsOne. https://newsone.com/playlist/black-men-youths-who-were-killed-by-police/item/3747351

Nieto, Sonia. 2003. "Afterword." In *Making Race Visible: Literacy Research for Cultural Understanding*. New York, NY: Teachers College Press.

Nittle, Nadra Kareem. 2019. "Five Examples of Institutional Racism in the United States." ThoughtCo. https://www.thoughtco.com/examples-of-institutional-racism-in-the-u-s-2834624

Nosek, Brian, et al. 2007. "Pervasiveness and correlates of implicit attitudes and stereotypes." *European Review of Social Psychology* 18(1): 36–88.

Okonofua, Jason A. and Jennifer L. Eberhardt. 2015. "Two Strikes: Race and the Disciplining of Young Students." *Psychological Science* 26(5): 617–624.

Pacini-Ketchabaw, Veronica. 2014. "Postcolonial and Anti-Racist Approaches to Understanding Play." In *The SAGE Handbook of Play and Learning in Early Childhood*. London, UK: SAGE.

Paley, Vivian Gussin. 1979. *White Teacher*. Cambridge, MA: Harvard University Press.

Paley, Vivian Gussin. 1994. "Princess Annabella and the Black Girls." In *The Need for Story: Cultural Diversity in Classroom and Community*. Urbana, IL: National Council of Teachers of English.

Paris, Django. 2012. "Culturally Sustaining Pedagogy: A Needed Change in Stance, Terminology, and Practice." *Educational Researcher* 41(3): 93–97.

Park, Caryn. 2011. "Young Children Making Sense of Racial and Ethnic Differences: A Sociocultural Approach." *American Educational Research Journal* 48(2): 387–420.

Partenio, Ingrid, and Ronald Taylor. 1985. "The Relationship of Teacher Ratings and IQ: A Question of Bias?" *School Psychology Review* 14(1): 79–83.

Payne, B. Keith, et al. 2010. "Implicit and Explicit Prejudice in the 2008 American Presidential Election." *Journal of Experimental Social Psychology* 46(2): 367–374.

Pettigrew, Thomas. 2008. "Future Directions for Intergroup Contact Theory and Research." *International Journal of Intercultural Relations* 32(3): 187–199.

Pew Research Center. 2015. "The Rise in Dual Income Households." Pew Research Center. http://www.pewresearch.org/ft_dual-income-households-1960-2012-2/

Phellas, Constantinos, Alice Bloch, and Clive Seale. 2012. "Structured Methods: Interviews, Questionnaires, and Observation." In *Researching Society and Culture*. 3rd ed. London, UK: SAGE.

Pianta, Robert, Michael Steinberg, and Kristin Rollins. 1995. "The First Two Years of School: Teacher-Child Relationships and Deflections in Children's Classroom Adjustment." *Development and Psychopathology* 7(2): 295–312.

Pigott, Rowan, and Emory Cowen. 2000. "Teacher Race, Child Race, Racial Congruence, and Teacher Ratings of Children's School Adjustment." *Journal of School Psychology* 38(2): 177–195.

Portman, Joel, Tuyen Trisa Bui, Javier Ogaz, and Jesús Treviño. n.d. *Microaggressions in the Classroom.* Denver, CO: University of Denver Center for Multicultural Excellence. http://otl.du.edu/wp-content/uploads/2013/03/MicroAggressionsInClassroom-DUCME.pdf

Powell-Hopson, Darlene, and Derek Hopson. 1988. "Implications of Doll Color Preferences among Black Preschool Children and White Preschool Children." *Journal of Black Psychology* 14(2): 57–63.

Quintana, Stephen, et al. 2006. "Race, Ethnicity, and Culture in Child Development: Contemporary Research and Future Directions." *Child Development* 77(5): 1129–1141.

Raabe, Tobias, and Andreas Beelmann. 2011. "Development of Ethnic, Racial, and National Prejudice in Childhood and Adolescence: A Multinational Meta-Analysis of Age Differences." *Child Development* 82(6): 1715–1737.

Ramey, Craig. 2018. "The Abecedarian Approach to Social, Educational, and Health Disparities." *Clinical Child and Family Psychology Review* 21(4): 527–544.

Ramos, Manica F., and Sarah Shea Crowne. 2019. "Home Visiting and Early Childhood Education Can Benefit Families by Broadening Their Strategies for Family Engagement." ChildTrends. https://www.childtrends.org/home-visiting-early-childhood-education-benefit-families-broadening-strategies-family-engagement

Rector-Aranda, Amy. 2016. "School Norms and Reforms, Critical Race Theory, and the Fairytale of Equitable Education." *Critical Questions in Education* 7(1): 1–16.

Richeson, Jennifer, Sophie Trawalter, and J. Nicole Shelton. 2005. "African Americans' Implicit Racial Attitudes and the Depletion of Executive Function after Interracial Interactions." *Social Cognition* 23(4): 336–352.

Rizvi, Fazal. 1993. "Children and the Grammar of Popular Racism." In *Race, Identity, and Representation in Education*. New York, NY: Routledge.

Rotheram, Mary Jane, and Jean Phinney. 1987. "Introduction: Definitions and Perspectives in the Study of Children's Ethnic Socialization." In *Children's Ethnic Socialization: Pluralism and Development*. Newbury Park, CA: SAGE.

Rugh, Jacob, and Douglas Massey. 2014. "Segregation in Post-Civil Rights America: Stalled Integration or End of the Segregated Century?" *Du Bois Review: Social Science Research on Race* 11(2): 205–232.

Sacks, Vanessa, David Murphey, and Kristin Moore. 2014. "Adverse Childhood Experiences: National and State-Level Prevalence." Research Brief. Child Trends. https://www.childtrends.org/wp-content/uploads/2014/07/Brief-adverse-childhood-experiences_FINAL.pdf

Sawhill, Isabel, Scott Winship, and Kerry Grannis. 2012. *Pathways to the Middle Class: Balancing Personal and Public Responsibilities*. Washington, DC: Center on Children and Families at Brookings, Brookings Institution. https://www.brookings.edu/wp-content/uploads/2016/06/0920-pathways-middle-class-sawhill-winship.pdf

Schuman, Howard, et al. 1997. *Racial Attitudes in America: Trends and Interpretations*. Rev. ed. Cambridge, MA: Harvard University Press.

Schweinhart, Lawrence, et al. 2005. *Lifetime Effects: The High/Scope Perry Preschool Study through Age 40*. Ypsilanti, MI: HighScope Press.

Semaj, Leahcim. 1980. "The Development of Racial Evaluation and Preference: A Cognitive Approach." *Journal of Black Psychology* 6(2): 59–79.

Shelton, J. Nicole, Tessa West, and Thomas Trail. 2010. "Concerns about Appearing Prejudiced: Implications for Anxiety during Daily Interracial Interactions." *Group Processes and Intergroup Relations* 13(3): 329–344.

Shockley, Kmt, and Rona Frederick. 2010. "Constructs and Dimensions of Afrocentric Education." *Journal of Black Studies* 40(6): 1212–1233.

Sinclair, Stacey, Andreana Kenrick, and Drew Jacoby-Senghor. 2014. "Whites' Interpersonal Interactions Shape, and Are Shaped by, Implicit Prejudice." *Policy Insights from the Behavioral and Brain Sciences* 1(1): 81–87.

Sinclair, Stacey, et al. 2005. "Social Tuning of Automatic Racial Attitudes: The Role of Affiliative Motivation." *Journal of Personality and Social Psychology* 89(4): 583–592.

Skiba, Russell, Robert Michael, Abra Nardo, and Reece Peterson. 2002. "The Color of Discipline: Sources of Racial and Gender Disproportionality in School Punishment." *The Urban Review* 34(4): 317–342.

Slavin, Robert, Nancy Madden, and Barbara Wasik. 1996. "Roots and Wings: Universal Excellence in Elementary Education." In *Bold Plans for School Restructuring: The New American Schools Designs*. Mahwah, NJ: Lawrence Erlbaum Associates.

Smith, Emilie P., Jacqueline Atkins, and Christian Connell. 2003. "Family, School, and Community Factors and Relationships to Racial-Ethnic Attitudes and Academic Achievement." *American Journal of Community Psychology* 32(1–2): 159–173.

Smitherman, Geneva. 2000. *Talkin' That Talk: Language, Culture, and Education in African America*. London, UK: Routledge.

Smitherman, Geneva, and Victor Villanueva, eds. 2003. *Language Diversity in the Classroom: From Intention to Practice*. Carbondale, IL: Southern Illinois University Press.

Stangor, Charles, ed. 2000. *Stereotypes and Prejudice: Essential Readings*. Philadelphia, PA: Psychology Press.

Steele, Claude, Steven Spencer, and Joshua Aronson. 2002. "Contending with Group Image: The Psychology of Stereotype and Social Identity Threat." In *Advances in Experimental Social Psychology*. Vol. 34. San Diego, CA: Academic Press.

Stevenson, Harold, and Edward Stewart. 1958. "A Developmental Study of Racial Awareness in Young Children." *Child Development* 29(3): 399–409.

Stevenson, Howard. 2018. "Vignette: Raisins in the Sun: White Teacher as a Force of Nature Buffering the Radiation of Racial Retaliation." In *The Guide for White Women Who Teach Black Boys*. Thousand Oaks, CA: Corwin.

Swanson, Dena Phillips, et al. 2008. "Racial Identity Development during Childhood." In *Handbook of African American Psychology*. Thousand Oaks, CA: SAGE.

Taie, Soheyla, and Rebecca Goldring. 2017. *Characteristics of Public Elementary and Secondary School Teachers in the United States: Results from the 2015–16 National Teacher and Principal Survey First Look*. NCES 2017-072. Washington, DC: National Center for Education Statistics, US Department of Education. https://nces.ed.gov/pubsearch/pubsinfo.asp?pubid=2017071

Tajfel, Henri, and John C. Turner. 1986. "The Social Identity Theory of Intergroup Behavior." In *Psychology of Intergroup Relations*. Chicago, IL: Nelson-Hall.

Teaching Tolerance Project and Southern Poverty Law Center. 1997. "Starting Small: Teaching Terminology and Practice." *Educational Researcher* 41(3): 93–97.

Teaching Tolerance Project and Southern Poverty Law Center. 1997. *Starting Small: Teaching Tolerance in Preschool and the Early Grades*. (Film and teacher guide.) Montgomery, AL: Southern Poverty Law Center. https://www.tolerance.org/classroom-resources/film-kits/starting-small

Tenenbaum, Harriet R., and Martin D. Ruck. 2007. "Are Teachers' Expectations Different for Racial Minorities than for European American Students? A Meta-Analysis." *Journal of Educational Psychology* 99(2): 253–273.

Todd, Andrew R., Austin J. Simpson, Kelsey C. Thiem, and Rebecca Neel. 2016. "The Generalization of Implicit Racial Bias to Young Black Boys: Automatic Stereotyping or Automatic Prejudice?" *Social Cognition* 34(4): 306–323.

Towles-Schwen, Tamara, and Russell Fazio. 2003. "Choosing Social Situations: The Relation between Automatically Activated Racial Attitudes and Anticipated Comfort Interacting with African Americans." *Personality and Social Psychology Bulletin* 29(2): 170–182.

Tropp, Linda, and Robyn Mallett. 2011. *Moving beyond Prejudice Reduction: Pathways to Positive Intergroup Relations*. Washington, DC: American Psychological Association.

Tversky, Amos, and Daniel Kahneman. 1974. "Judgment under Uncertainty: Heuristics and Biases." *Science* 185(4157): 1124–1131.

Umek, Ljubica Marjanovic, Simona Kranjc, and Urska Fekonja. 2000. *Child Development in the Context of Multicultural Pre-School Education*. Report. Ljubljana, Slovenia: University of Ljubljana. https://files.eric.ed.gov/fulltext/ED450957.pdf

US Census Bureau. 2018. "Population." Quick Facts. https://www.census.gov/quickfacts/fact/table/US/RHI125218#RHI125218

US Census Bureau. 2015. "America's Families and Living Arrangements: 2015." US Census Bureau. https://www.census.gov/data/tables/2015/demo/families/cps-2015.html

US Department of Education. 2011. "Obama Administration Releases Final Application for Race to the Top-Early Learning Challenge." US Department of Education. http://www.ed.gov/news/press-releases/obama-administration-releases-final-application-race-top-early-learning-challeng

US Department of Education. 2015. "Digest of Education Statistics 2015, Table 203.50." Institute of Education Sciences, National Center for Education Statistics. https://nces.ed.gov/programs/digest/d15/tables/dt15_203.50.asp

US Department of Health and Human Services, Administration for Children and Families. 2019. "Head Start Timeline." Head Start Early Childhood Learning and Knowledge Center. https://eclkc.ohs.acf.hhs.gov/about-us/article/head-start-timeline

US Department of Health and Human Services, Administration for Children and Families, Office of Head Start. 2011. *The Head Start Parent, Family, and Community Engagement Framework: Promoting Family Engagement and School Readiness, from Prenatal to Age 8*. Arlington, VA: Head Start Resource Center. https://cyfar.org/sites/default/files/cyfar_research_docs/Parent%2C%20Family%2C%20and%20Community%20Engagement%20Framework%20Promoting%20Family%20

Engagement%20and%20School%20Readiness%20from%20Prenatal%20to%20Age%208.pdf

US Department of Education Office for Civil Rights. 2016. *2013–2014 Civil Rights Data Collection: A First Look*. Washington, DC: US Department of Education Office for Civil Rights. https://www2.ed.gov/about/offices/list/ocr/docs/2013-14-first-look.pdf

US Department of Education Office for Civil Rights. 2014. *Civil Rights Data Collection: Data Snapshot (School Discipline)*. Washington, DC: U.S. Department of Education Office for Civil Rights. https://ocrdata.ed.gov/Downloads/CRDC-School-Discipline-Snapshot.pdf

Van Ausdale, Debra, and Joe Feagin. 1996. "Using Racial and Ethnic Concepts: The Critical Case of Very Young Children." *American Sociological Review* 61(5): 779–793.

Van Ausdale, Debra, and Joe Feagin. 2001. *The First R: How Children Learn Race and Racism*. Lanham, MD: Rowman and Littlefield.

Violent Crime Control and Law Enforcement Act of 1994. 1994. 18 U.S.C. § 3559(c).

Walton, Gregory, and Geoffrey Cohen. 2007. "A Question of Belonging: Race, Social Fit, and Achievement." *Journal of Personality and Social Psychology* 92(1): 82–96.

Wang, Qi, and Michelle Leichtman. 2000. "Same Beginnings, Different Stories: A Comparison of American and Chinese Children's Narratives." *Child Development* 71(5): 1329–1346.

Weinstein, Rhona, Anne Gregory, and Michael Strambler. 2004. "Intractable Self-Fulfilling Prophecies Fifty Years after *Brown v. Board of Education*." *American Psychologist* 59(6): 511–520.

Weiss, Heather B., M. Elena Lopez, and Margaret Caspe. 2018. "Joining Together to Create a Bold Vision for Next-Generation Family Engagement: Engaging Families to Transform Education." Global Family Research Project https://globalfrp.org/Articles/Joining-Together-to-Create-a-Bold-Vision-for-Next-Generation-Family-Engagement-Engaging-Families-to-Transform-Education

Williams, Amanda, and Jennifer Steele. 2019. "Examining Children's Implicit Racial Attitudes Using Exemplar and Category Based Measures." *Child Development* 90(3): e322–e338.

Williams, John, et al. 1975. "Preschool Racial Attitude Measure II." *Educational and Psychological Measurement* 35(1): 3–18.

Wing Sue, Derald. 2010. *Microaggressions in Everyday Life: Race, Gender, and Sexual Orientation*. Hoboken, NJ: John Wiley and Sons.

Zenou, Yves, and Nicolas Boccard. 2000. "Racial Discrimination and Redlining in Cities." *Journal of Urban Economics* 48(2): 260–285.

Zepeda, Marlene, Carrie Rothstein-Fisch, Janet Gonzalez-Mena, and Elise Trumbull. 2012. *Bridging Cultures in Early Care and Education: A Training Module*. New York, NY: Routledge.

Zigler, Edward, and Jeanette Valentine, eds. 1979. *Project Head Start: A Legacy of the War on Poverty*. New York, NY: Free Press.

Zigler, Edward, Walter Gilliam, and W. Steven Barnett, eds. 2011. *The Pre-K Debates: Current Controversies and Issues*. Baltimore, MD: Brookes.

INDEX

recognizing, 58

religious, 4

sexuality, 4

Black children. *See* Children of color.

Black Feminist thought, 96

Black History Month, 80

Black lives

impact of institutional racism, 26–28

lost to police shootings, 25–26

Black Lives Matter movement, 87

Black teachers, 54–55

Bold Plans for School Restructuring
(Stringfield et al.), 85

Bridging Cultures in Early Care and Education
(Zepeda et al.), 60–61

Brown v. Board of Education, 43

Burden of educating Whites, 48–49

C

Carolina Abecedarian Project, 10–13, 113

Child Care and Development Block Grant,
10

Child Care and Development Fund, 10

Child-care assistance, 11

Children of color, v–vi

adultification bias, 58–59

experience more ACEs, 33–34

impacts of institutional racism, 26–28

implicit biases about, 2–5

institutional racism and, 16–17

majority of public school students, 20–21

perceptions of, 4, 6, 27–28, 51–53

racial self-identification, 91–92

suspension and expulsion rates, 31–32

workplace diversity, 54–55

Children's books, 64–65

Children's racial attitudes, 89–91

ethnographic data review, 94–95

historical and contemporary review, 91–94

race and intersectionality, 95–102

Child-to-staff ratios, 9

Citizenship status, 42–43

Civil rights movement, 56

Class bias, 4

Classroom environment, 71–72, 76

Afrocentric, 100–101

Cognitive development, vi, 5, 10, 106

challenges, 32

identity threats and, 52–53

Collectivist perspective, 60–63

Color-blindness, 91

Controlling racial bias, 47–50

The CRAF-E4 Family Engagement Model
(Iruka et al.), 107

Critical race theory, 96

Cultural Awareness Inventory (Boehman),
43

*Cultural Competence in Early Childhood
Education* (Curenton & Iruka), 84

Cultural diversity

children's awareness of, 63–65

classroom environment, 71–72, 76

empathy, awareness, and prejudice, 65–67

importance in classroom, 59–63

individualism vs. collectivism, 61–63

Culturally relevant pedagogy, vi–vii, 51–53,
70–71, 80–81

anti-bias education and, 80–81

children's social-cultural awareness, 63–65

conceptions of knowledge, 71

conceptions of self and others, 70

culture and, 59–63

empathy, cultural awareness, and internalized
prejudice, 65–67

example of, 71–75

research support for, 57–67

social relations, 71

Culture Matters (Durden et al.), 84

F

Family engagement, 9, 12–13, 73–75

    4Es, 107–109

    defined, 104–112

    example, 109–112

    frameworks, 105–106

    linking to social justice, 112–115

    resources for, 114–115

Feeding skills

    individualist vs. collectivist, 62

Flint, Mich., water crisis, 35

Foster care, 29

Frank Porter Graham Child Development Institute, 10

G

Gender bias, vii, 53, 58

Global Family Research Project, 114

Goals, 78–80

Graduation rates, 10

H

Hate crimes, 46

Head Start, 4, 108, 113

    Parent, Family, Community Engagement Framework, 8–9, 106

    role in equitable learning opportunities, 5–6

Health development, 5

    addressing needs, 12–13

    impact of early childhood education, 10

High expectations, 70, 107

HighScope Perry Preschool Program, 10, 113

Hispanic children. *See* Latinx children

Homophobia, 58

Households headed by grandparents, 28–29

Housing discrimination, 8

Human-Centered Design (Global Family Research Project), 114

Hypersensitivity, 35

I

Identity development, vi, 58, 91–92

Identity threats, 52–53

Immigrant families, 108

Immigration policies, 28–29, 87

Implicit bias, v–vii, 27

    reality of, 2–5

    defined, 3–4

Implicit racial bias, 45–47

    controlling, 47–50

    defined, 45

Individualist perspective, 60–63

Institutional racism, 16–17, 19–40, 100

    impact on Black lives, 26–28

    implications for early childhood professionals, 28–40

    recognizing, 58

    three-strikes laws, 23–25

Internalized prejudice, 65–67

Intersection of race and ACEs, 31–36

Intersection of race and opportunity, 36–40

Intersection of race and program quality, 29–30

Intersectionality

    defined, 95

    observing for, 99–102

    race and, 95–102

Police shootings of minorities, 25–26

Poverty, 5, 14, 29, 32, 34–35

    achievement gaps, 7–8

    intersection with opportunity, 36–40

    race and, 36

Prejudice, 93

    internalized, 65–67

Preschool Racial Attitude Measure
    (Williams et al.), 93

Privilege walk, 39–40

Pro-Black attitudes, 93–94

Professional development, 13

Program considerations, 83–85

Pro-White attitudes, 93–94

Q

QRS Learning Network, 115

R

Race to the Top–Early Learning Challenge
    grant (RTT–ELC), 12–13

Race

    and intersectionality in children's lives,
    95–102

    intersection with ACEs, 31–36

    intersection with opportunity, 36–40

    intersection with program quality, 29–30

Racial awareness, 91–92

    defined, 92

Racial bias, v–vi, 4, 9, 28, 44–50, 58

    addressing in preschools, 10–13

    among children, 91–94

    controlling, 47–50

    explicit, 46–47

    implicit, 45–47

    institutional. 16–17, 19–40, 58, 100

"Racial innocence," 90–91, 101

Racial language, 97

Racial self-identification, 91–92

    defined, 92

Racism. *See* Racial bias

Recognizing unfairness, 78

Redlining, 8

Reflection activities

    challenge your perceptions, 53

    getting Black teachers into the pipeline, 55

    "I Am From," 82–83

    Lemonheads and Whoppers, 49–50

    privilege walk, 39–40

    "Where I'm From," 85

Reflection questions

    anti-bias education, 75, 77, 87

    children's racial attitudes, 101–102

    family engagement, 114

    social justice, 9, 15

    understanding racial bias, 50

    white privilege/institutional racism, 22, 28

Religious bias, 4

S

Say What? (University of Nebraska
    Extension), 85–86

Segregation, vi, 42–43, 46

    de jure vs. *de facto*, 43

Self-awareness, 81–83

Self-regulation, vi, 13, 32, 36

Sexism. *See* Gender bias

Sexuality bias, 4

Single-parent households, 28–29

Slavery, 8, 26, 42

Small group size, 9, 28

Social cognition, 63, 65

Social identities, 52–53

    defined, 52

Social justice

    Carolina Abecedarian Project, 9–13

    defined, 7–8

    education, 103–115

    family engagement, 104–112

    Head Start's role, 5–6

    HighScope Perry Preschool Program, 9–10

    linking family engagement to, 112–115

    preschool suspension and expulsion, 14–17

    roots in early childhood education, 1–17

    War on Poverty and, 7–9

Social-cultural awareness

    children's, 63–65

    empathy and internalized prejudice, 65–67

Social-emotional development, 5, 10, 13, 106

    challenges, 32

    misperceptions and, 51

Sociodramatic play, 97–100

Southern Poverty Law Center, 85

Starting Small (Teaching Tolerance & Southern Poverty Law Center), 85

Storytelling, 55

    Afrocentric, 101

    Eurocentric, 16–17

    written vs. oral, 16–17

Structural racism. *See* Institutional racism

Student-teacher relationships, 70, 85–86

Substance abuse, 14, 34

Substance abuse programs, 108

Suspension and expulsion, 58, 85

  Black vs. White children, 2–5, 14–17, 31

T

Teachers

    challenging misperceptions, 43, 51–53

    diversity, 43, 54–55

    role in children's lives, 42–43

    self-awareness, 81–83

    understanding racial bias, 43–50

    well-paid, well-trained, 9, 13

Teaching credentials, 13

Teaching Tolerance Project, 64, 78, 85

Theory of the mind, 66

Three-strikes laws, 23–25

Tourist curriculum practices, 75–76, 80

Toxic stress, vi

Trauma

    lifelong impact, vi–vii, 14

Trauma-informed care, 15–16

    defined, 14

Tribalism, 47–50, 87–88

U

Unconscious biases. *See* Implicit biases

Underachievement, 51

University of Nebraska, 85–86

US Census Bureau, 20, 23, 29

US demographics

    changing, 20–21, 23

    implications for early childhood professionals, 28–40

    teachers and students, 42, 54–55

    US Dept. of Education, 3, 12, 20–21, 29–32, 58

    National Household Education Survey, 104

US Dept. of Health and Human Services, 8, 12

V

Violent Crime Control and Law
   Enforcement Act, 23

VISTA. *See* AmeriCorps VISTA

W

War on Poverty, v, 2, 5

   early childhood education, 7–9

"Where I'm From" by George Ella Lyon, 82

White privilege, 16–17, 19–40, 91, 95

   defined, 21–22

   implications for early childhood
      professionals, 28–40

   observing for, 97, 102

   recognizing, 58

   three-strikes laws, 23–25

White-nationalism, 46

Workplace diversity, 54–55

X

Xenophobia, 58